CAGNEY

CAGNEY

THE STORY OF HIS FILM CAREER BY MINTY CLINCH

PROTEUS BOOKS, LONDON AND NEW YORK

Proteus Books is an imprint of
the Proteus Publishing Group

United States
PROTEUS PUBLISHING CO., INC.
733 Third Avenue
New York, N.Y. 10017

distributed by:
THE SCRIBNER BOOK COMPANIES, INC.
597 Fifth Avenue
New York, N.Y. 10017

United Kingdom
PROTEUS (PUBLISHING) LIMITED
Braemar House
Sale Place
London, W2 1PT

ISBN 0 86276 060 7 (paperback)
0 86276 061 5 (hardback)

First published in the U.S. 1982
First published in the U.K. 1982

Design: by Mary Dunkin
Editor: Chris Goodwin
Typeset by Wordsmith Graphics, Street, Somerset BA16 0LQ

Printed by Printer Industria Grafica sa, Barcelona, Spain
D.L.B. 29275—1982

CONTENTS

ROOTS
8
SONG AND
DANCE MAN
16
SHOOTING
TO KILL
24
TOP DOG
48
ONCE
A SONG
AND DANCE
MAN...
74
INDIAN
SUMMER
90
FARMER JIM
112
BACK IN
HARNESS
118
FILMOGRAPHY
124

CHAPTER 1
ROOTS

17 July 1899: to James Francis and Carolyn
Nelson Cagney, a second son.

Uncharacteristically, in the light of the eighty
years of grim purpose and impeccable health that
were to follow, James Francis Cagney Junior was
born mewling and puking, a sickly infant whose
twenty-year-old mother feared for his life. As a
good Catholic, she also feared that he would die
without being baptised and so be barred from
heaven. She need not have worried for young
Jimmy, as he was always called, survived the crisis
and never looked back.

The Cagneys were first-generation Americans,
the children of European immigrants. Carolyn's
mother was born in County Leitrim in 1846 to
parents who were soon obliged by the potato
famine to cross the Big Pond in order to survive.
Her father, Henry Nelson, came from Drobak in
Norway, a sailor whose globe trotting eventually
brought him to roost along the waterways on the
Eastern Seaboard of the United States as captain
of a barge carrying coal and lumber. He was, by
all accounts, a colourful character with a leonine
head of hair and an unbreakable habit of laying
into people when he was in his cups. It was a
game he rarely came out of ahead but his
irrepressible aggression, inherited by Carolyn and
young Jimmy, was to stand the family in good
stead.

Turn-of-the-century New York was no place for
cowards or fools. It was one of the melting pots of
the world, the destination of an unending stream
of Europeans fleeing from prejudice and poverty
to the crock of gold at the end of the rainbow.
Many of the immigrants passed on to wider
pastures but others, especially Italians and Jews,
stayed right where they got off the boat and
moved into Manhattan's teeming Lower East
Side. The Irish, who had been arriving in droves
over the past half century and were already well
established in these territories, felt the wind of
change and imminent deprivation. They had no
intention of playing second fiddle to spics and
spivs, still less to the negroes who were moving up
from the South in the aftermath of the Civil War.
Trouble was never far away.

With Lois Calhern and Noel Francis in *Blonde Crazy.*

The Cagney foothold on mainland America was precarious to say the least. Little is known about James Cagney Senior's antecedents except that he was descended from the O'Caigne's of County Leitrim, but his life-long absorption with bars and bookmakers mark him as a true Irishman! His most famous son remembers him as a lovable, feckless man: 'Pop's gentle waywardness was thorolly engrained. He had the charm of the Irish minstrel — he did everything to the tune of laughter — but he was totally deficient in a sense of responsibility to his family. Despite this, he always thought he was doing well for us. At times, things got very rough. At best he had a spotty job record: here a job, there a job, and long stretches of nothing in between.'

The early days in Hollywood.

In the event, he would have been better employed almost anywhere else but in a saloon and indeed at times he worked as a bookkeeper but bars, whichever side of them he was on, exercised a fatal attraction. At one stage, he even owned his own, only to fritter away the asset on slow horses and fast women. After his death. cheque stubs to his bookmaker for such astronomical sums (in those days) as 150 and 200 dollars were found among his effects, clear proof that Jimmy's childhood need not have been as deprived as it undoubtedly was.

That neither his wife nor his offspring resented their breadwinner's erratic ways is almost certainly due to his capacity to make them laugh. His tricks and mannerisms, mighty threats and broad guffaws and, above all, his overt physical affection held Carrie, as he called his wife, and the kids in thrall so that he was assured of a warm

welcome, even though the hearth was cold for lack of fuel.

Nevertheless it was fortunate for Jimmy and his brothers that their mother was made of sterner stuff. She was, in her son's eyes, a raving beauty with titian hair hanging a foot below her waist. At the age of twelve, poverty in the Nelson family had forced her to leave school to work in a factory belonging to the Eagle Pencil Company, and it was this curtailment of her own very promising studies that made her vow that she'd get her boys an education come what may. As she had four of them — Harry, a year older than Jimmy, Eddie, born in 1902 and Bill, born in 1904 — this was no easy task but she set about it in the right way, by instilling in them the sense of family responsibility her husband so dramatically lacked.

Cagney recalled that Carrie was a mother twenty-four hours a day. That was her job and she devoted herself to it totally. She made herself into a protective shield between the harsh environment of the streets and her sons. But she also brought them up to understand what was going on around them so that they could build their own defences against corruption. Ugliness, crime and vulgarity paid dividends in ugliness, crime and vulgarity, but not to her sons while she had breath left in her body.

This deep understanding of the conditions her children would face in the streets was one of the secrets of Carolyn's remarkable success as a mother. She knew that in a rough neighbourhood it didn't do to turn and run and she herself, armed with a six-foot horsewhip, would defend her brood against injustice with the blazing fury of a tigress defending her cubs. Not for nothing was her hair flaming red. On one occasion, Jimmy remembers, his elder brother Harry had been wrongly beaten up by a nightwatchman in revenge for a prank practised on him by a local gang. Enter Carolyn, with whip, on the rampage; exit the watchman, howling.

This combative attitude became increasingly necessary as Jimmy's childhood progressed. In his early years, East Seventy-ninth Street (on and off the Cagney base) was a wide thoroughfare with brownstone flats occupied by sensible working people, but by 1912 the dope pushers had arrived and the area deteriorated rapidly. Cocaine was hard currency and with it came organised crime, rival groups of gangsters who would shoot each other as soon as pass the time of day. Jimmy went to school with their sons, and fought them afterwards as and when occasion demanded, and that was pretty often. It was not so much a liking for fisticuffs, more a way of life demanded by a neighbourhood in which the pecking order was decided by brute force.

Cagney senior, a good boxer and a competent ballplayer in his youth, bequeathed his short,

stocky frame and natural athlete's grace and ease of movement to all four of his sons, but only Jimmy and Bill inherited Carolyn's retaliatory nature as well. From his very early years, Jimmy's titian head could be seen in the thick of any scrap which demanded an honourable solution. He was ever ready to plunge right in against towering opponents in order to avenge his brothers, even the older and taller Harry to whom fighting didn't come at all easily.

'There was almost a kind of chivalry about street fighting in our neighbourhood,' he commented. 'If two fellas were fighting on the street and one fella was getting badly beaten he could nominate someone else to take his place. Mind you, you could wind up with a shiner that way if you got in the wrong league. Sometimes it didn't pay to be that chivalrous! Don't think my street fights were wild scrambles though. I knew how to box from the age of six when a mature neighbourhood boy showed me how to jab, feint, hook left, cross with a right, and a hook — the business. I used to work out with real fighters and one pro gave me extended training in things I already knew basically.'

While he was still at high school, one of Jimmy's mates made ten dollars in a preliminary bout and he, with an eye on the family budget, thought he might have a go as a professional. Then, as now, pro boxing was a well trodden route out of the ghetto, but Jimmy had reckoned without his mother. Carolyn, noting her son training ferociously and losing weight rapidly on a sugar-free diet, asked the reason why and received the reply that he could 'make ten bucks easily because he could lick most of the fellas without strain.' 'Well, that's just fine,' she answered, 'but can you lick me?' Knowing full well he couldn't, his fine hopes drained away.

Though he had a passion for drawing and reading, young Jim's achievements in school varied according to where his parents were living at the time. Carolyn ran her educational programme on competitive lines, offering a dollar a month to the son who had the best report. When the family moved out to the Long Island suburb of Ridgewood, Jimmy, an ace speller, had no trouble securing the prize but back in East Seventy-ninth Street, his straight A's reverted to B's and C's. Still he always reckoned that there was more to school than book learning and that his time in the classroom wasn't wasted. If the subject didn't interest him, he would doodle in the margins, catching the movements and expressions of the children around him, observations that were to stand him in good stead in his screen career.

The Cagney family was always close-knit, united against the outside world by Catholicism and pride. They went to church on Sundays, dressed in their best clothes, and to religious instruction on Tuesdays, and Carolyn made sure they lived up to what they were taught. They were poor but they were honest. Often they didn't get three square meals a day and there was never any question of having a good second suit but they were never turned out of their house for not paying the rent. They lived at subsistence level from day to day, hoping to get through the bad times with as little hunger as possible. Nor was their poverty, in a neighbourhood notable for its desperation, in any way unique.

But there was never any chance of the four Cagney boys enjoying the luxury of an uninterrupted education. Each had to have evening and weekend jobs to make ends meet, not for things they might have wanted to buy for themselves, but to finance the communal kitty. Even before Cagney senior, weakened by booze, succumbed in two days to the 'flu epidemic in 1918, aged forty-one, leaving Carolyn pregnant with Jimmy's much younger sister, Jeanne, the older boys were holding down regular part-time jobs.

Jimmy's first, when he was fourteen and still at Stuyvesant High School, was as a junior architect; his second as a copy boy on the New York Sun. After school and on Saturdays, the diminutive figure would struggle uptown with vast bundles of the newspaper under one arm and rolls of advertising proofs under the other to deliver to department stores for correction. The reward for this grinding toil was a paypacket of five dollars a week which he gave to his mother unopened — and with considerable pride.

A year later he was to be found, along with Harry and Eddie, in the New York Public Library replacing books on their correct shelves for twelve-and-a-half dollars per month for a twenty-two-and-a-half hour week. When he was sixteen he was promoted to custodian, earning himself a princely rise of five dollars monthly. In the holidays, the pace was even more intense. During one vacation, Jim wrapped bundles at Wanamaker's department store during the day, then transformed himself into a switchboard operator and attendant at a pool hall in the evening. He'd be up until three a.m., racking balls and acting as an unofficial 130lb. bouncer. On Sundays he sold tickets for the Hudson River Day Line. He reckons that all this activity was good for him because kids who have a cushy childhood have a much tougher time when they finally have to face up to reality.

Fortunately for Jimmy, his brothers were as conscientious as he was so he didn't have to carry the load alone. Harry, a natural athlete with a fine track record in swimming, diving and running, entered Columbia Medical School the year his father died, only to have to leave it to recoup the family finances before he'd graduated. His tutor,

saddened by the decision, said that no one ever came back in such situations but Harry, with typical Cagney grit, proved him wrong by qualifying in 1925. Eddie, dubbed the family wit from very early days when he would chip in with one-liners that creased everybody up, followed in Harry's footsteps but Bill, a born entrepreneur who was selling cauliflowers door to door round the flats where the Cagneys lived from the age of eight, was clearly cut out for big business. He was also an ace pool and poker player and it came as no surprise to anyone when he grew up into an ace salesman. Much later, when Jimmy wanted to set up his own production company, it was Bill he picked to manage it.

'Our motto was united we stand, divided we fall,' Cagney once said in an interview. 'I can't remember a time when, if any one of us had three bucks, he didn't throw it immediately into the kitty. We never thought of doing anything else. Boys who worked for their own pocket merely were beyond our understanding. And doing things together, working for the common end, sharing everything, as Mother drummed into us, instead of each going off in separate directions gave us the feeling we were strong. The trouble with most poor families is that they don't have that community of feeling and alone they're helpless in a tough world.'

The one thing that set young Jimmy way apart from his brothers and his parents was his extraordinary love and appreciation of the countryside. Coming from a poor city family, he had few opportunities to see green fields and breathe fresh air but when he did, one happy day of prosperity when his father scraped together the wherewithal to hire a barouche and take his offspring for a fortnight's holiday at the home of a great-aunt, he was bowled over. Nowadays the area his aunt lived in, the part of Brooklyn called Flatbush, not far from Kennedy Airport, could hardly be described as rural but at the turn of the century, it was open farming country — and Jimmy was overwhelmed.

'The vivid memory is with me yet,' he wrote many years later. 'I can still see the tremendous elm in her front yard and the morning glories crowding the white picket fence. Ever since those two glorious weeks, morning glories have been my favourite flower and, just as lasting in its effect, during those few days I changed from a city boy into a country boy. When I retured to Seventy-ninth Street after two weeks of freedom in the golden air, I was indescribably saddened. It is enough to say that I have loved the country ever since, totally.'

Carolyn, along with the rest of the Cagneys, retained her preference for urban grime but she wasn't one to fail to provide encouragement for any respectable passion, however strange she

Punching the keys.

might find it. If her second son preferred farms to thoroughfares, so be it. When he was eleven, she took him to hear a lecture on birds and the often detrimental effect they were having on the American countryside, so introducing him to conservation and its other face, the rape of the land which became, overnight as far as Jimmy was concerned, a much graver crime than any he saw daily in Manhattan's tawdry streets.

Again at his mother's suggestion, he wrote off for further information to the Farmingdale School' of Agriculture — and avidly awaited the arrival of the literature through the mail. Instead it was brought by a puzzled employee whose experience of New York families was negligible but who certainly hadn't expected his target audience to be a small red-headed boy, let alone one who devoured his arid pamphlets on soil erosion and conservation before his very eyes. From that day forward, Jimmy resolved to be a farmer but it was an ambition he would be some time in fulfilling.

It is hardly surprising that at no time in his childhood did he express any interest in acting. Vaudeville was the order of that day and, in an age of nickelodeons and silent one-reelers, the noble profession of film actor had barely been invented. Yet, bit by bit, though quite unconsciously, he was using his natural talents to built up the equipment and skills that would characterise his performances in so many films to come.

Like his father, he only grew to five feet eight inches, with a compact, highly mobile and muscled physique that he developed through those countless street brawls into a well co-ordinated fighting machine. It was equally useful for amateur boxing competitions in which he was runner-up for the New York State lightweight title and for semi-professional baseball which he played for the Original Nut Club of Yorkville. Their programme included exhibition matches in prisons, among other institutions, where Cagney sometimes encountered members of local gangs who'd fallen foul of the law. In his very musical family, there was no shortage of song and dance routines and Jim, a natural when it came to tap dancing on angled boards, soon found himself nicknamed, 'Cellar-Door Cagney'.

It is probably relevant, when considering his

screen charisma, that he always seems to have stood out in a crowd, partly because of that celebrated titian hair, inherited from Carolyn, that earned him another more long-lasting nickname, 'Red'. He has often said that his aggressive behaviour was nothing special in its context and that to earn a reputation, you had to be able to throw a decent punch. It was just a way of being a 'hell of a fella', a vital adjunct of not being pushed around. Yet neighbours seem to have remembered the young Jimmy as a firebrand, a hyper-aggressive boy who was always fighting, something that surprises him considerably. It is possible, of course, that by the time anyone cared enough to ask their opinion twenty years on, Jimmy's fame as a screen gangster had added sparks to their recollections.

Mentally he was extremely observant and sensitive to other people's accents and mannerisms. As life's rich pageant could hardly have been richer than down the Cagney's way, his opportunities for mimicry were boundless. These lessons he learnt very well as he acknowledges in his autobiography. 'The polyglot nature of my neighbourhood is the basic reason why all my life I've had such an appreciation and understanding of dialects. I ought to — I was surrounded by them. Indeed, I was twenty-two before I ever met an elderly man who spoke without an accent, and when I heard this fella speak I was actually startled.'

The Cagney boys had plenty of opportunities to pick up all sorts of phrases from the Germans, Czechs, Italians and Jews they shared their

Home movies, with his wife and brother.

writing poetry) rather than the gun, was brought up among gangsters. Many of the drinkers in his father's saloon were men of the kind his son would immortalise in celluloid. Jimmy, who visited the premises frequently, knew how such people behaved, how they moved and how they talked. The next generation sat beside him in class, boys who would kill cops and land up in Sing Sing. Among them was his friend Bootah who hung by his fingertips from rooftops five storeys above street level to show how brave he was, only to die young in the electric chair in 1927.

Jimmy absorbed all this material like a sponge, storing it against the days he would need it, although he was totally unaware of the possibility at the time. But why, you may ask as he has often been, did none of the young Cagneys succumb to the easy pickings of Manhattan's East Side as so many of their contemporaries did?

'The answer is simple: there wasn't a chance,' Jimmy is wont to reply. 'We had a mother to answer to. If any of us got out of line, she just belted us, and belted us emphatically. We loved her profoundly, and our driving force was to do what she wanted because we knew how much it meant to her. We loved the great staunchness in her, and at times we four brothers together would impulsively put our arms around her, hold her and hug her. She'd look at us, her nose would get red, and she'd start to cry. She just couldn't take all that love.'

And so, in 1918, instead of pushing dope or clouting opponents round a boxing ring for filthy lucre, Jimmy enrolled in the Student Army Training Corps at Columbia University where the drawing skills he'd been developing since he was six were in demand in the camouflage unit. It was here too that the oral reading class pinpointed another Cagney speciality that was destined to become world famous. The professor, appalled by Jimmy's rat-a-tat-tat delivery, tried to slow him down. Fortunately for posterity he did not succeed!

Despite all this invaluable grounding, there was little sign at this stage that Jimmy was to be the Cagney who would take the cinema by storm. He had toyed with the idea of medicine but rejected it while Harry and Eddie forged ahead with their studies and Bill too was well set on his chosen course. So when the family finances once again had to be urgently recouped in the aftermath of the war, Jeanne's birth (an event that was marred by snide comments from the neighbours as to her paternity) and Cagney senior's death, it fell to Jimmy to give up his studies in order to put groceries on the table. Back he went to tying parcels at Wanamaker's but this time it was not a long-term sentence, for fate — and his mother — were about to take a decisive hand.

classrooms with. Jim prided himself on being a good German student but, as 90 percent of his fellow scholars were Jewish, he also learned the Yiddish equivalent. In later life, he spoke some German but a lot more Yiddish. This no doubt would have distressed his German teacher, Mr. Mankiewicz (the father of Joseph L. Mankiewicz who was later to join Cagney in Hollywood as a famous writer and director) but the Yiddish, which Jim often used for sure-fire comic effect in his pictures, turned out to be the greater asset in the long run.

When it comes to mannerisms, it is worth remembering that Jimmy, who throughout his life has wielded the pen (both for sketching and for

CHAPTER 2
SONG AND DANCE MAN

It was in 1919 that Jim first trod the boards, and pretty humble they were too. They belonged to the Lenox Hill Settlement House, a multi-activity club for people of all ages who lived in the area. Carolyn had decreed that Harry's medical future could only benefit from his joining the dramatic society to improve his speech. For her second son, however, she preferred scenery painting in line with the liking for art he'd shown since he was six. Accordingly Harry acted as best he could while Jim painted, drew dance posters and designed the cover of the House's magazine.

So it might have continued except that Harry fell ill and his lookalike sibling was hurriedly conscripted to take his place. The experience wasn't a revelation, but it did interest Jimmy sufficiently for him to join the society and take a few parts in some of their productions. Distinguished they emphatically were not and, after playing in a Japanese musical comedy, an Italian harlequinade and a period costume melodrama, he reached rock bottom in a two-act play called *The Faun*. Cast in the title role with his hair in ringlets and the rest of him in a goatskin loincloth, he cavorted nimbly round the stage gabbling such inanities as 'The wayward wynd ran its fingers through the pine tree's hair . . .' Not surprisingly, the erstwhile terror of the Lower East Side trod warily in the streets on the way home but fortunately the more abrasive local element were not theatre-goers.

Meanwhile at Wanamaker's he found himself wrapping and tying alongside a show business enthusiast who would while away the long boring hours by talking through his subject. His audience wasn't interested in the frills and furbelows: he needed a job that paid more and the store wasn't the place to find it. Among other things, they discussed The Peabody (an intricate dance named after the Boston cop who'd invented it) which represented the sole Cagney hoofing achievement at the time. He'd been taught it at the Lenox Hill Settlement and, with his natural speed and ability to mimic movement, he had it off pat. On hearing of this skill, his friend told him about Keith's Eighty-first Street Theatre where they were look-

In his early stage success 'Women Go On Forever'.

16

ing for a sixth 'chorus girl' for a vaudeville show called *Every Sailor*. The pay was thirty-five dollars a week, more than double the Wanamaker wage. Jim needed no second invitation.

The act was a hang-over from the First World War that had done the rounds of naval bases to keep morale up during breaks in hostilities. Now, with Jim as one of the six 'guys in skirts', it had a few last New York audiences to go for before fading into well-deserved oblivion. 'It was a knockabout act, purely burlesque,' Cagney remembered. 'We had a lot of fun and it never occurred to any of us to be ashamed of it. It might seem strange and unbelievable taking into account my habitual desire to go unnoticed. But again this illustrates what I mean when I say that I am not shy or selfconscious when I am on the stage or screen. For there I am not myself. I am not that fellow, Jim Cagney, at all. I certainly lost all consciousness of him when I put on skirts, wig, paint, powder, feathers and spangles. Besides, that was the time when service acts were still fresh in mind, when female impersonators were in vogue.'

Jimmy himself admits that he faked the dancing part at first, that he was ever ready to stand and stare while the pros got on with it so he could steal their steps. In fact the only training he had throughout his career was from observation.

When the show died its natural death. Carolyn, who hadn't been over-impressed with her son's new occupation, re-routed him into more respectable, though deadeningly dull, work as a runner for a brokerage house but the theatre was beginning to get into Jim's blood. Then and throughout his career, it wasn't the burning desire to act that took him from production to production but the realisation that here was a way to earn more money for less drudge.

In the aftermath of war people were hell bent on pleasure and the foundations of riches to come were being laid in all kinds of new fields, from advertising and public relations to liquor running during Prohibition. Society was fluid and anyone who was 'upwardly mobile' could take a crack at the big time with a real prospect of hitting the jackpot. As far as entertainment went, vaudeville, in its last great decade, held good on the East Coast while the silent cinema, now well established in the reclaimed desert known as Hollywood, was producing its early masterpieces and its first authentic superstars — and paying them accordingly.

Although Jimmy was only dimly aware of all this, he defied his mother for one of the few times in his life to join another chorus line, a boys' one this time, on a Broadway show called *Pitter, Patter* which opened in the Longacre Theatre in September, 1920. He won the part from fifty rivals, replying, when asked if he could sing and dance, 'Sure, I can' with all the assurance of a one-show trouper. The production was mediocre, a musical adapted from a farce called *Caught in the Rain*, but the set-up offered openings for commercial acumen. Before long Jimmy was adding fifteen dollars a week to his basic thirty-five for dressing and understudying the star. When the show went on the road, he was able to lay claim to a further ten bucks for looking after the baggage. All this represented riches beyond the dreams of avarice to Carolyn, and her opposition to his play-acting drained away. Better still the management fired the other seven chorus boys and Jim was promoted to speciality dancer.

Even that was not the best thing that *Pitter Patter* had to offer James Cagney for the show also marks Carolyn's replacement as the lady in his life by the girl who was to become his one and only wife. Frances Willard Vernon was on the girls' chorus line, a dark-haired smiling lass standing a suitably diminutive five feet one inch. She'd run away from her home in distant Iowa to take her chance in show business. As the sixth daughter of a man who had always wanted a son, she was nicknamed 'Billie' which Jim abbreviated still further to 'Bill'. Although she was warmly recommended to him by his best friend on the show, he was wary of asking her out because he was afraid she'd eat into the family budget by demanding sirloins and champagne.

How wrong he was. Bill was to stand by him through thick and thin, and during the next ten years of his life while he was trying to establish himself, it was certainly mostly thin. As they were both working together, their introduction was inevitable and it came one lunchtime when they were grabbing sandwiches over a counter between rehearsals. Later a doorman, seeing them chatting, asked Jim if he was going to take her out. He was just explaining that he didn't have any money when Bill, having overhead the exchange, chipped in with 'I'll pay'. Going Dutch wasn't normal form on a first date in 1921 and her unorthodox behaviour won the money-conscious Cagney heart. Soon the pair were inseparable and, when *Pitter Patter* closed after thirty-two weeks, they were married.

'The show was fairly unmemorable,' Jim recalled, 'except that I met the great girl who became my wife. I can't conceive of how lucky a guy can get but this lady and I have celebrated more than fifty years of marriage and it's been joy all the way. My Bill and I hit it off from the beginning. Marrying her was the smartest thing I ever did in the whole course of my life and I'm still crazy about the lady.'

In 1922, Billie, who had an 'instinctive gift of rhythm' according to her husband, was much the better known, and the couple had no doubts about setting up their own vaudeville act. They called it Vernon and Nye (a re-arrangement of the last three letters of Cagney) and they hawked it around without ever looking as if they'd set show biz on fire.

Their routines were simple and mawkish. There was, for example, 'Out of Town Papers' in which Billie played the provincial girl who meets Jimmy's streetwise newspaper seller on a corner in New York, only to discover that he comes from the same small town where she was born. The coincidence flings them into a joyful song and dance routine with Billie singing 'Home Sweet Home' and Jim counter punching with 'That's Broadway'.

Naturally people weren't queuing up for such drivel, particularly in the southern states where no one understood a word of Jim's gunfire gabble. His youngest brother, Bill, occasionally took his place in the audience and even he was embarrassed as he later admitted: 'I used to swell up with pride when Jimmy came out to dance. The kid was a pretty fair hoofer. I'd look round and tell anyone who'd listen, 'Say, that's my brother. Good ain't he?'. But dancing would never satisfy him. I could always feel it coming. He'd edge down to the footlights and a baby spot would pour pink light on him. Then Jimmy would sing. Boy, I sunk down in my seat then and I wanted to be out of the way when they started throwing things.' Jim denies he was that bad and reassures himself with the thought that they never threw *rotten* vegetables at him.

The great American public wasn't much more impressed with Lew Fields' Ritz Girls, a travelling show which took the Cagneys to St Louis in 1922 — and dumped them there when the funds dried up. As Mr Fields' creditors had seized the players' salaries, only a wealth of aggressive cross talk with the backers in New York got them their fares back to base.

More fiascos followed and the couple reached rock bottom when they found themselves in Chicago with just seventeen dollars to their name. That was just enough to buy Billie a ticket back to Manhattan where she found a job in vaudeville while Jim was otherwise ungainfully employed in downtown Detroit. Her show closed after seven weeks of unpaid rehearsal and just three performances. His never got off the ground at all. It was much the same story with *Dot's My Boy,* a sickening play in which Jim was cast as a Jewish lad who danced on stage watched by his proud parents. When the clapping started, his mother stood up and cooed, 'dot's my boy' which was Jim's cue to recite a poem about mothers.

By 1924 Billie's mother had moved to California so it seemed like a good idea to go to the West Coast to meet her and to explore the possibilities of breaking into the movies at the same time. No dice. As Cagney's speech played such a vital part in his later film performances, it is possible that he wouldn't have shown to his best advantage in silents but the Hollywood producers never gave him a chance to prove it one way or the other. The great iron studio gates remained firmly locked against the Cagneys. Jim was too short and too red-headed, they said, though why that should have mattered in the days of black and white was never explained to him. In desperation they opened a dance studio in a hired rehearsal hall, only to find that their first pupil, a highly proficient Scotsman who'd been condemned by casting moguls as 'too ungainly', knew much more than his putative teacher.

The Cagneys rented a tiny house in Los Angeles for thirty-five dollars a month. They had virtually nothing to live on but Billie managed to provide for them. They even gained weight. However, as their attempts to break into pictures failed, they began to get hints that it might be better to go back East. Billie found she was being reproached for marrying a song and dance man who couldn't earn a living, and an alien New Yorker at that. Go back where you belong, was the message, and as weeks turned to months, it came over increasingly loud and clear.

So they acted on it, having wired a journalist friend in New York for money for the fare. There the struggle continued. When he wasn't half of Vernon and Nye Jim was a third of Parker, Rand and Cagney, having replaced Archie Leach, no less, in the three-man vaudeville team. 'Archie who?' you may be asking and with reason for he is now much better known as Cary Grant. When Jim joined up, 'Variety', among others, was not impressed: 'Two boys and a girl with a skit idea that gets nowhere. It is a turn without the semblance of a punch. There are no laughs and the songs mean little. One of the boys (Cagney) can dance a bit. Small time is its only chance. Trio gets 275 dollars tops.'

And a third of that, even when Jim got it, was never enough, especially as he was still sending money home to help Carolyn and Jeanne whenever he could. Throughout the first half of the twenties, the Cagney fortunes were chronically unstable. Jobs came slowly and went quickly and they often had to borrow money. Bill, who had made good in advertising, was always ready to help out when work was scarce or non-existent. Jim would hang out on the corner of Forty-seventh Street where theatrical gossip gave hints of jobs on offer. Most of his rivals looked on themselves as specialists and would only answer calls to auditions in their own fields, but Jim was prepared to try anything and to exaggerate his skills so as to get himself hired above other, probably better prepared, candidates. Of course he often got fired but he reckoned that such varied experience stood him in good stead, not

least because he became battle-hardened in a profession where sticking in there is the only way of winning the war.

Vaudeville also taught him to analyse what really pleases. The material was generally slight so its presentation was vital. A slight movement here, a shade of a tone there made the difference between making an audience laugh and laying an egg. Cagney watched and listened and learned from the experts, borrowing and mimicking and perfecting his techniques. That great vaudevillian George M. Cohan may not have thought much of his talent when he passed him up at an audition but the reverse was not true. However Jimmy had the last laugh twenty years later when he gave the greatest performance of his film career as Cohan in *Yankee Doodle Dandy*, winning his only Oscar in the process.

By 1925, when his career was about to make its first quantum leap with his first major dramatic role in a play called *Outside Looking In,* Jim had proved that he was as gutsy a fighter in adversity as he had been in the streets of the Lower East Side but, as he freely admits, he might never have stayed in the business long enough to make good, had it not been for his wife.

'In the midst of all that hardship of jobs gained, jobs lost, jobs deferred, jobs lousy, jobs few, there was always the wonder of my Bill,' he said, with evident sincerity. 'I'm obliged by sheer facts to say that the rock-solid honesty and sterling character of this little gal made possible our going comparatively unscathed through the years when we were in dire straits. It was rough. At times no food in the larder, big holes in the shoes. When I didn't have a penny, she was out working. Life seemed just a never-ending sequence of damned dingy badly furnished rooms with a one-burner plate.'

She wouldn't let him quit though he was often tempted by the lure of a weekly pay cheque. Maybe he had to sweep the stage here and there and fill in with odd demeaning jobs, but give up? Billie wouldn't hear of it. As far as she was concerned, her husband had talent and eventually people who mattered would recognise it.

The first who did was a young agent called Max Arnaud who put Jim forward for *Outside Looking In*, a play about the writer-hobo Jim Tully, written by Maxwell Anderson. The producer wanted a 'fresh young mutt' and hit upon Jimmy's in the crowd of young hopefuls at the audition, as he sat perspiring freely on the radiator in a ploy to disguise his lack of inches. His role was 'Little Red' opposite Charles Bickford's 'Oklahoma Red' and he always claims he got it because his hair was redder than that of any of his rivals. The

George Kelly's play 'Maggie the Magnificent'.

play opened at the 299-seat Greenwich Village Playhouse on September 8, 1925, and later switched to the much more spacious Thirty-ninth Street Theatre. At last Jimmy was on Broadway.

At this point people started to sit up and take notice, among them Robert Benchley, at that time the drama critic for *Life*, who wrote: 'Wherever Mr MacGowan (the director) found two redheads like Charles Bickford and James Cagney, who were evidently born to play Oklahoma Red and Little Red, he was guided by the hand of the casting God. Mr Bickford's characterisation is the first important one of the year and is likely to remain at the top for some time, while Mr Cagney, in a less spectacular role, makes a few minutes silence during his mock-trial scene something that many a more established actor might watch with profit.' The play ran for four relatively well-paid months and Jim hoped for a follow-up to establish himself as a dramatic talent. Instead he was obliged to return to Parker, Rand and Cagney and the humiliations of the vaudeville circuit.

Six months later the next halfway decent offer came through, to appear on the London stage in George Abbott and Phil Dunning's *Broadway*, a smash hit production currently raking audiences in New York. The leading character in the gangster melodrama was Roy Lane, a song and dance man who gets involved with mobsters, a part Cagney should have been a natural for. He'd been passed over during the initial casting in favour of Lee Tracy, an excellent actor who couldn't dance for nuts. However the London production wasn't far behind New York and the sailing date was fixed. There was even a dancer's role for Billie. Not surprisingly Jimmy believed he had it made.

The dress rehearsal had taken place before an audience of 1,000 (followed by riotous applause for Cagney's Roy Lane), the farewell party had been thrown and the Cagney luggage stowed in the liner's hold when the bad news came through. The producers, who had always demanded that Jim should model himself on Lee Tracy (something he'd conscientiously attempted but failed to do because Tracy was 'an ungainly fella'), had decided to replace him at the very last moment. Instead he was condemned to understudy Tracy in New York. It was a bitter blow, and one that influenced Billie's decision to withdraw from show business out of dislike for the politicking and backbiting that permeated it. Jim, too, thought long and hard about going on with it at this point but, with his wife's staunch support, decided that he couldn't quit while he was behind.

In 1927 he thought he'd finally got a serious part in a serious play, Daniel Rubin's *Women Go On For Ever*. That anyway was what it was supposed to be but doubts were raised when its star, Mary Boland, trying to go straight after years of success as a comedienne, had her first line greeted by gales of laughter. After that,

Keeping in shape — somewhat wistfully.

though the play lasted eighteen weeks, it never in any way reflected its writer's original intentions. Cagney's performance, however, received special praise from the 'Morning World' critic, Alexander Wollcott, so it was another brick in the frail reputation he was slowly building for himself.

Curiously, it was at this time that he had a second crack at opening a dancing school, having presumably learnt nothing from his Los Angeles venture. The Cagné School of Dance in Elizabeth, New Jersey was equally disastrous financially although it appears to have attracted a few more students. He taught there during the day, gulped down two giant containers of pineapple juice and headed at full speed for the theatre for *Women Go On For Ever*, an exhausting programme which he was glad to give up the next year when he found himself in a popular topical revue.

The Grand Street Follies 1928 gave Jim the opportunity to stage several of his own dance numbers and to hoof it to his heart's content, especially in a stunning tango tap finale. He played in most of the sketches and the whole thing worked out well for him. 'Among the other features of the revue worth noting' wrote Stephen Rathbun of the 'New York Sun', 'were a comical burlesque of talking pictures, the Spanish dancing of Sophia Delza and the American dancing of James Cagney.' *The Grand Street Follies 1929*, also at the Booth Theatre, followed naturally but the gilt had fallen off the gingerbread, always a danger in a follow-up. As one unfavourable reviewer put it, 'It has all the sophistication and verve of an 1884 Almanac on a rainy afternoon in the Louvre.'

Audiences agreed with this somewhat delphic opinion and it was as well for Jim that they did for the show closed quickly, leaving him free to take up a part in *Maggie the Magnificent*, written and directed by George Kelly. Even more fortunately he caught the great man's eye during casting. 'I looked out through the stage door,' the maestro told his protégé some months later, 'and I saw you in the crowd of actors waiting there and asked that you be sent in directly. You were just what we were looking for — a fresh mutt.'

Another fresh mutt in the production was that of Joan Blondell, also a high flyer in the making. She took an instant shine to Cagney but, on being invited along with the rest of the cast to a lunch hosted by Billie and seeing the lovelight in Jim's eyes, she realised she was in a no-go area emotionally. Not that her stage sparring partner was oblivious to her charms for he commented, 'One of several good things about the play was that I met that delightful trouping lady, Joan Blondell. I played a young heel and Joan was the character comedienne, all gum-chewing and wisecracks and sidelong glances. I also must say I noted at the time that she had a perfectly beautiful body, something my bride knows I've said a number of times.'

Professionally they clicked instantly and their duo as a smart-talking floosie and her boyfriend was the highlight of the production. It opened at the Cort Theatre to mixed notices, only to close thirty-two performances later, partly because of the Stock Market crash in October, 1929, which took the bottom out of the leisure business, among others.

However the word about Cagney and Blondell had got around and one of those who had heard it was William Keighley, then top of the Broadway hierarchy. A couple of months later, when he was casting Marie Baumer's *Penny Arcade*, he thought of Jim for Harry Delano, the rotten-to-the-core offspring of Arcade-keeper Ma Delano, and of Joan for Myrtle, the girl who is Harry's paid alibi after he murders his boss. The play was routine melodrama, its carnival setting serving to emphasise the brutality of the story line, and the critics panned it. However they found time and space to praise Cagney. 'Theatre' magazine wrote: 'Mr Cagney is giving an excellent performance as the weak amoral son and his confession of the crime to his mother stands out as the high point of the play.'

Penny Arcade had even shorter legs than *Maggie the Magnificent*, shutting its doors after just twenty-four performances but among those who'd got to see it was Al Jolson, rich and famous as the star of the first talkie, *The Jazz Singer* which he'd made in 1927. Self-styled as 'the World's Greatest Entertainer' after the biggest ever cinema box-office hit, his confidence was unbounded and his instinct for hit material thought to be invincible, not least by himself. On the opening night, he bought *Penny Arcade* for 20,000 dollars, re-selling the film rights to Warner Brothers by phone the next day.

When he spoke to Darryl Zanuck, the Burbank Studio boss had to sit up and take notice and this is what he heard: 'I've just seen the greatest play they've ever had on Broadway and I know something about that street. And I'll tell yer, it'll make the swellest movie too.'

To which he added, 'I won't let it go unless you have the two Broadway leads too. They're the sharpest couple of kids I've ever seen. A gal called Joan Blondell. The fella's James Cagney.'

Zanuck squirmed and wriggled at the thought of fresh mutts but finally, in deference to his hottest property, he capitulated. Warner Brothers sent a three-week contract at five hundred dollars a week and the aggressive redhead from the Lower East Side headed west once more. Prudently, remembering the last time, Billie stayed at home to see how things would work out. She needn't have worried for Hollywood, apparently, was ready for James Cagney.

CHAPTER 3
SHOOTING TO KILL

He came, he saw, he conquered, and he stayed for thirty-one years, making sixty-two films, more than half of them in the Thirties. It was lucky he arrived when he did because vaudeville was dying on its feet back home while talkies were producing queues around blocks around the world at the start of the cinema's most exciting decade.

Not that Joan and Jim's first slice of the action set the world on fire. When they first arrived in the Zanuck empire, the youthful mogul toyed with the idea of giving them rather larger parts than the ones they'd played in New York, but changed his mind after screen tests as it seemed safer. That was Jim's first introduction to Hollywood's percentage philosophy by which something that's worked once can be repeated ad infinitum. It was a way of thinking that was to drive James Cagney mad.

As a new boy, though, he had to conform, so he resumed as Harry Delano in *Penny Arcade,* duly re-christened *Sinner's Holiday* in line with a vogue for titles with 'holiday' in them. The film, which was completed in the three weeks of Jim's contract and ran for just under an hour, introduced audiences to the Cagney they were to come to know and love: a gangster with a mother, trademarks that would mould his career. It is unlikely that Jim found much physical resemblance to Carolyn in Lucille La Verne, the raw-boned farm-type woman who played the penny arcade keeper, Ma Delano, but her staunch defence of her delinquent son, even after she learns that he has accidentally murdered his liquor baron boss, must have struck chords. As a result, the climactic scene in which Harry breaks down into infantilism in her lap is touchingly pathetic, especially when constrasted with his normal jauntiness. 'Don't cry. You know I love you,' he comforts her when he is finally led away in handcuffs. It is the start of something big with mothers, culminating nineteen years later in *White Heat.*

The first Cagney gangster also sets a precedent with the audience feeling compassion for the hapless delinquent on the grounds he couldn't help it because his father was a hopeless alcoholic. In the light of his own and his brothers'

The Public Enemy.

experience, Jim could hardly have subscribed to that soft option but his portrait is entirely convincing. 'It is less a picture of action than of character, made so by the skill of Lucille La Verne and James Cagney,' wrote 'Time' magazine, in rare favourable comment, while Mordaunt Hall of the 'New York Times' said, 'The most impressive acting is done by James Cagney in the role of Harry Delano. His fretful tenseness during the closing scenes is conveyed with sincerity.'

Warner's, pleased with their new acquisition, signed him up for a second three-week contract at five hundred dollars a week, then for forty weeks at four-hundred-and-fifty dollars a week, peanuts even then in the embryo movie business but sufficient security for Billie to join her husband. In his next picture, *Doorway to Hell*, he was given the second lead as the quiet pal opposite Lew Ayres's big-shot hood, the one who stabs his friend in the back by seducing his girl and taking over his territory. This time the role is not softened by social excuses and Cagney plays it nasty, proving to his employers that he was the

stuff that gangsters are made of.

The film started slowly but built at the box-office and very little time passed before the cameras were turning on Jim in William Well-man's *Other Men's Women* in which he gives a short vulgar performance as the friend of the railroad worker hero. The film was a dud but it gave Cagney his first opportunity to flash off a few dance steps in a brief inspiring sequence. His part in *The Millionaire* was even shorter, a three minute stint as an insurance salesman to George Arliss's retired millionaire. Yet, in that brief time span, Cagney changed the fictional course of the

Upstaging the experienced George Arliss in *The Millionaire* (1931).

older man's life and, incidentally, the factual course of his own.

'If I was a man like you, you know what I would do?' he asks Arliss. 'Well, I wouldn't sit around and wait for an undertaker.' It is the shot in the arm the suave old man needs, delivered in rapid-fire clipped phrases. Jim wore a pinstripe suit and a white hat as he addressed his prey, confined to a wheelchair, in his garden, and what an impact he made, brashly upstaging the experienced Arliss in the process. 'That was my only scene with this great star,' he said, 'and I wanted it to be good.'

It was, and it established another characteristic in the emerging Cagney film persona, the fast talker, which studio and directors soon came to depend on in all Jim's roles. Warner's knew a good thing when they saw it and ordered Jim to report for duty on a new film called *The Public Enemy*, with which they hoped to repeat the triumph of *Little Caesar*, their top scorer of 1930.

Originally they planned to cast Cagney as the quiet Matt Doyle and Eddie Woods as the cocky Tom Powers and there is a certain amount of Hollywood myth about who suggested the final solution. The writers Kubec Glasmon and John Bright claimed they always wanted Cagney for the lead but Jimmy himself recalls that it was director William Wellman who thought the casting was 'ass backwards' and made the switch on the basis of having seen his performance in *Doorway to Hell*.

'He knew at once that I could project that direct gutter quality so Eddie and I changed roles after Wellman made an issue of it with Darryl Zanuck,' said Jim, but Jack Warner saw it differently. 'We gambled that Cagney, who was a sort of bonus rookie, could deliver when the pressure was on,' he recalled.

The mantle of Tom Powers, once it had firmly settled on Jim's shoulders, was to do for him what Rico had done for Edward G. Robinson in *Little Caesar*: make him an international star. At the start, though, no one was particularly aware of that. The script, based on a story called 'Beer and Blood', concocted by newspapermen Glasmon and Bright from the life of a Chicago Prohibition-beater called Tom Druggan, was run of the mill

The Public Enemy (1931). Left, a moment of romance with Jean Harlow; below, Mae Clark on the receiving end of the blow that launched a thousand grapefruits.

gangster stuff. In Tom Powers it has a Mr Average urban hero, a youth from a poor but honest background who is fatally attracted by the lure of easy money into becoming a lawbreaker who dances to the commands of Putty Nose, his gangland boss.

If art is a reflection of life, then Hollywood was right to pick on Prohibition, and the ingenious ways of getting around it, as the central theme of so many of its Thirties pictures. After all, many an American had spent the dry Twenties either engaged in that nefarious activity or reaping its illicit benefits. *The Public Enemy* has an ingenious booze heist, using a petrol tanker to rob a warehouse, that shows the lengths bootleggers were prepared to go to to please their public behind the closed doors of speakeasies nationwide.

Cagney's Tom Powers is dynamite, a juvenile delinquent who graduates, along with his pal, Matt Doyle, to rum-running, despite the sorrowful request of his mother (Beryl Mercer) and his brother (Donald Cook) that he should quit. No way, says Tom, who enjoys broads and booze and snappy dressing. Not that he's all bad. He's prepared to share the proceeds with his family, even with the toffee-nosed war hero brother, because he loves them. And his mother, another comfortable body, loves him despite everything.

Up to this point, the ingredients of Jim's part were similar to those in *Sinner's Holiday*. He talked fast, moved fast and led the more impressionable Matt into the cesspool of big city corruption until they were both out of their depths. But there were two things about *The Public Enemy* that set it apart from the gangster films that preceded it: its hero's treatment of women and its ending. Throughout the silent era, women had been portrayed as fragile as porcelain, delicate creatures to be wooed with voiceless passion by Valentinos and Fairbanks. They were sex objects on pedestals, pure and unattainable out of wedlock, and as such were invariably addressed with gentlemanly decorum.

By the Thirties, the mood had changed towards a greater realism and most gangsters were allowed their molls. They weren't seen to go to bed with them but that they did was implicit in the story. A degree of rough treatment was acceptable but things had never gone so far as they would in *The Public Enemy*'s most famous scene in which Cagney, newly risen after a hard night, squashes his breakfast grapefruit in Mae Clarke's face. As his mistress, she'd been over-indulging in a little unwise early morning wingeing. 'Maybe, you've found someone you like better?' she enquires. Tom Powers' answer is unequivocal. He picks up the fruit, thrusts it forward and twists it deftly as it hits flesh, a totally contemptuous gesture not only to Mistress Mae, but to all

womankind.

Once again the scene's antecedents are obscure, with people connected with the picture hurrying to claim the credit. This time too Wellman gets most peoples' votes. Cagney had this to say about the thrust that launched a thousand gift grapefruits in his direction: 'When Mae Clarke and I played the scene we had no idea that it would create such a stir. That grapefruit was to become a piece of Americana. It was just about the first time, if not the very first, that a woman had been treated like a broad on the screen, instead of like a delicate flower.'

The grapefruit sequence was inspired by a real

With Eddie Woods, his partner in crime in *The Public Enemy.*

wanted so in the end Jim gave up eating the intrusive fruit in public altogether.

Glasmon and Bright confirmed the Hymie Weiss origins but Darryl Zanuck preferred his own version, that he thought the whole thing up at a script conference. However Wellman's statement, made at an interview some years later, that the idea sprang from a long-nurtured urge to smash his own wife in the face during breakfast — just as a joke, he claimed — has the ring of truth about it! The man made most happy by the incident seems to have been the unfortunate Mae Clarke's husband, Monty Brice (Fanny's brother), who never missed a screening of the film, coming in nightly just before the sequence to gloat and leaving directly afterwards. All this ensured that Mae Clarke, rather than Joan Blondell (once again sharing the credits with Cagney) or the young and insipid Jean Harlow, has been immortalised as the woman in Tom Powers' life.

Not that she was too happy about it. 'I'm sorry I ever agreed to do it,' she said some time afterwards, having found herself relentlessly typecast due to the fifteen-second incident. 'I never dreamed it would be shown in the movie. Director Bill Wellman thought of the idea suddenly. It wasn't even in the script. As for Cagney, he is an old pro. He knows how to pull his punches. The grapefruit just glanced off my face. We needed just one take for the scene.'

Equally startling is the ending in which Tom, having tried to avenge Matt's death at the hands of rival gangsters, is wounded and hospitalised. Trussed up in bandages, he makes his peace with his mother and agrees to return home but, as she is cheerfully making his bed in anticipation of his arrival, the doorbell rings to reveal a roped blanket-wrapped figure that pitches forward into the house. Tom Powers is well and truly dead and crime is not the best way out of the gutter as the epilogue, with a wary eye on the Hays Office whose business it was to keep a check on burgeoning violence in the movies, assured the public.

In Britain, the film was mysteriously rechristened *Enemies of the Public.* Not that that prevented it from being banned for a year, and when it was finally shown, the grapefruit scene, along with several others, had been left on the censor's cutting room floor. Even the sound of the gunshot that killed the horse was taken out, a silent homage to the supposed sensibilities of a nation of animal lovers.

The picture, which cost 151,000 dollars and took just twenty-six days to make, was one of the first multi-million dollar grossers, an overnight sensation that put the name of James Cagney on everybody's lips. Certainly it broke new ground and some of its other scenes, notably Tom Powers'

life incident in Chicago when a gangster called Hymie Weiss got fed up with his girlfriend's chatter one breakfast time and shoved an omelet she'd just made straight into her face. Obviously an omelet was a trifle messy for the film so the grapefruit was enlisted instead. At one time Cagney despaired of ever living the scene down. For years, whenever he went to a restaurant, some joker would order the waiter to bring over a tray of grapefruit. Often there was hardly enough room on the table for the dishes they really

His one appearance with Edward G. Robinson, in *Smart Money* (1931).

rain dance, after the ill-fated revenge shootout, in which he clutches his stomach and moans, 'I ain't so tough,' are memorable but Jim never believed that he'd hit the jackpot overnight with *The Public Enemy*, let alone that his fame was anything more than transitory.

It was left to others to recognise his talent, including, some years later, Kenneth Tynan who analysed *The Public Enemy* with his customary astuteness: 'Cagney presented for the first time, a hero who was callous and evil, while being simultaneously equipped with charm, courage and a sense of fun . . . The result was that in one stroke he abolished both the convention of the pure hero and that of approximate equipoise between vice and virtue.' Cagney, according to Tynan, was the face of the Thirties, a desperate decade of bread lines and Depression, largely because he was so resilient he would always fight back, no matter how great the horrors or the odds. Above all he'd smile while he was doing it.

There is no doubt that *The Public Enemy* marked Jim's transition from hack to superstar but, hog tied as he was by his Warner's contract, it made very little difference to his life. He continued to earn his four-hundred-and-fifty dollar weekly pay cheque and to report on demand for whatever the studio had to throw at him. Yet

he hated his gangster parts for the very reason he played them so well, because he knew first hand how mobs operated and how urban corruption acted like a cancer in a poor community. He remembered the sad drunken figure of his father standing behind his bar and serving hoods; the schoolfriends who'd turned into juvenile delinquents like Tom Powers and ended up dead; the mothers, like Ma Powers, who'd feared and pleaded with their sons to go straight but hadn't had Carolyn's driving force and Irish temper to insist on it.

Such knowledge made his tough-guy portrayals chillingly realistic but, given his intrinsically gentle nature, it was inevitable that he sympathised at least as much with Will Hays and his protective attitude towards movie audiences as with the cynical exploitative Jack Warner. His own life was exemplary. Although his brothers, appalled by their father's example, had taken the pledge, Jim never went that far. As he didn't much like alcohol, he never drank it to excess but he was prepared to sip an occasional glass of champagne when he went to the studio parties he hated so much. As for smoking, he claims he

Learning to be a gentleman with Loretta Young in *Taxi* (1932).

never took it up, though he wasn't above making some fast bucks by appearing in newspaper advertisements for a certain brand of the filthy weed.

After work, he'd go home, content to be with Billie far from the madding crowds of Hollywood. He resented having to attend publicity exercises, especially for other people's pictures, or glittering premieres but, most of all, he resented having to toe the Warner's line. After *The Public Enemy*, the studio gave him star billing which pleased him but certainly didn't compensate for getting pushed around. He found he was required to grind the picture out at maximum speed and he didn't even get much appreciation for his efforts.

Actors were treated like dirt, as expendable as props or make-up, and for this the tough little Irishman eventually meant to have his revenge.

But, by 1931, after the meteoric rise that put him at the top of the cast list in just his fifth film, he wasn't in a position to do much about it. When the studio had the bright idea of teaming tops with tops, Edward G. Robinson with James Cagney, in *Smart Money*, it was business as usual. As Robinson was still ahead of Cagney, he got to play the hero, a greedy, amiable provincial barber with a penchant for gambling. Cagney was the pal

('It seemed to me I was playing an awful lot of pals those days'), the assistant barber who joins his boss when he moves to the big city in an attempt to win a huge fortune. When he succeeds and becomes a master games-player, the trouble begins and the police take an over-active interest in his career, leading inevitably to disaster.

This routine plot, written once again by Glasmon and Bright and directed at snail's pace by the plodding Alfred E. Green, is saved from total obscurity by the performance of its stars, the calm and unshakeable Robinson and the brittle mobile Cagney. Their styles are in splended contrast and it is a shame that they never had a chance to play together in a better vehicle. Otherwise the picture is only notable because Jim has a second opportunity to slap a lady in the kisser, screaming 'You dirty little stool pigeon' as he does it, so hammering another plank into his public platform as a masochistic tough guy. He may not, as he has always claimed, have said 'You dirty rat' to anybody but many of his lines weren't far enough removed from it to make any difference in the minds of his public.

Or in the minds of his promoters, as his next four films, made at lightning speed during 1931 and 1932 show. Warner's now knew they had something special on their hands and plugged their hard-boiled trouper to the hilt. As a result his career escalated and his fame spread. His roles varied from out and out brutal to likeable conman, broad-beater to gallant rogue, but they were generally law-defying and he was apt to end up dead.

The first of this quartet, *Blonde Crazy*, known as *Larceny Lane* in Britain, is Jim's first screen comedy and among the best of the seven films he made with Joan Blondell. They play a couple of con artists, a button bright bellhop and his feisty chambermaid friend, whose cross-country spree is financed by the cunning fleecing of suitable victims. It is a zany early road movie, fast moving and full of double entendres from a lively Glasmon and Bright script. For once the glove is on the other fist and Joan hammers Jim at every opportunity. However his masculine image is not affected, partly because comedy doesn't count and partly because he ripostes, 'I'd like to have you hit me like that every day.' Also in the film is a young newcomer called Raymond Milland who is addressed by Cagney as a 'dirty double-crossing rat', once again not too far removed from the rejected 'dirty rat'.

When *Blonde Crazy* boomed at the box office, Jim at last felt secure enough to stage the first of many walk outs. 'I realised that there were roughly two classes of stars at Warner's,' he recalled. 'Those getting 125,000 dollars a picture — and yours sincerely, who was getting all of four hundred dollars a week. And that four hundred soon stopped because I walked.'

Hollywood was outraged. In 1932, the studio bosses were dictators who literally tried to own their actors and they were quite unaccustomed to being crossed. Later Pat O'Brien, Humphrey Bogart, Bette Davis and George Raft would take their turns to walk off the Warner's lot but Cagney was the pioneer. He went straight back to New York. At first he said he'd leave show business altogether and become a painter, then that he'd return to Columbia University and study to become a doctor like Harry and Eddie. They weren't overjoyed at the prospect of welcoming their 'gangster' sibling into the respectable suburb of Queens where they had a joint practice, but Jim and Bille went anyway. In his home town, Cagney found he was a celebrity, greeted by streetwise people everywhere as a long lost brother, but pride in such a reputation didn't stop him getting off the transcontinental train at Grand Central Station and walking home.

Three thousand miles away, Warner's executives were chewing their pencils and wondering what to do. There was huge public demand for Cagney films and they had a contract binding him to churn them out on command but, for the first time ever, they were having problems enforcing it. They had reckoned without his basic reason for working. Whether as a teenager, a vaudevillian or a movie star, his often stated purpose was 'to put groceries on the table'. And they'd reckoned without his ferocious Irish obstinacy and sense of justice which told him that if there weren't enough groceries to make the job worthwhile, then it was time to quit.

After three months of irritable negotiations, the dispute was patched up and Jim was offered a contract at 1,000 dollars a week, with periodic reviews. Even at that price, and with the raises he extracted later, he was a gift to the studio which grossed a million dollars minimum from every film he made after 1934. What's more, Jim recognised the fact and went right on resenting it.

'I did a whole series of these walkouts over the years,' he remembered. 'I walked because I depended on the studio heads to keep their word on this, that or the other promise, and when the promise was not kept, my only recourse was to deprive them of my services.' He is proud of the fact that he never quit in the middle of a picture, a favourite ploy for some actors. He found considerable support for his position from his peers and some of them, infuriated by seven-year contracts which gave the studios total power over their lives, joined him. Only then did the dictatorship of management over talent begin to be broken.

As the studios had tremendous clout in the

In Howard Hawks' *The Crowd Roars* (1932).

courts, those who tried to fight back legally were apt to get stung and withdrawals of vital services gradually became common-place over the years. Safely back in the Warner's fold, Jim was enlisted for Roy del Ruth's *Taxi*, which had the bonus of allowing him to work with another then unknown New York hoofer. At that time George Raft was new to Hollywood and struggling but, when *Taxi* turned out to feature Jim's first and favourite step, the Peabody, he knew he needed another genuine vaudevillian as his main and ultimately victorious rival in a dance contest. Accordingly he persuaded the studio to sign up George, whom he'd known back home.

Taxi had a promising script (once again by the dependable Glasmon/Bright team) and a young capable leading lady in Loretta Young whose determination to make a gentleman out of the independent taxi drivers' leader (Cagney) is at the heart of the matter. This time Jim's part of the little fighting man pitted against the hoodlums of a massive taxi trust is less obnoxious but he still treats his screen wife with dismissive violence. However he considered this to be one of his more

sympathetic early films, if only because he isn't an out and out villain. Or he would have done, if it hadn't been for the driving and the bullets.

Before starting on the picture, he insisted he had to take driving lessons, something he'd never remotely wanted before. The Lower East Side was not exactly car territory and a man as careful of the cents as Jim wasn't about to rush out to buy himself a set of wheels when he was earning 450 dollars a week. In *Taxi* however he would have to drive so, with his customary determination to paddle his own canoe rather than rely on doubles,

he had to learn. On 1,000 dollars a week he could afford to buy a car and he did. From the first, when he drove on set, he hated it, especially the noise of the engine, augmented by the honking horns and urban pandemonium of the taxi war.

Even more dangerous were the bullets. This was before the discovery of harmless special-effects 'exploding' bullets and the only way to shoot someone up was to blast away for real. This had happened safely by virtue of split second timing in *The Public Enemy* but the margin on *Taxi* was even finer, as Cagney explained: 'I had an adventure bordering on misadventure. From my taxi I had to fire two shots out of the window and duck; then a machine gun would cut loose and take the window out over my head. The scene was played as called for with one exception: one of the machine-gun bullets hit the head of one of the spikes holding the backing planks together. It ricocheted and went tearing through the set, smacked through a sound booth, ripped across the stage, hit a clothes tree and dropped into the pocket of someone's coat. I was young enough not to consider this a pretty dangerous activity.'

Jim had to get behind the wheel again, in even noisier circumstances, for his next picture, one of Howard Hawks' more obscure works called *The Crowd Roars*, in which he was cast as a top racing driver with an over-riding compulsion to win. Yet another Glasmon and Bright screenplay, from a story based on ex-racing driver Hawks' own passion for the track, it brings out the self damage inflicted by too great a desire for victory but founders on a soggy romance which has a rejected sweetheart (Ann Dvorak) returning at the end to save her ruined loved one. Joan Blondell, as a Cagney kid brother's fiance, is the recipient of most of the physical rough stuff when she is grabbed by the scruff of her neck, called a tramp, knocked to the ground and marched out of the room, but the adoring Miss Dvorak comes in for her share of verbal abuse, leaving no doubt in the brainwashed public mind that the dapper speed-way merchant, Joe Greer, was a true Cagney hero.

Jim has always claimed that acting was just a job for him and that the only consolation for being ripped off by the studio financially and forced to hit women on behalf of characters he despised was the friends he made along the way. One of the best of these was Frank McHugh, the youngest of five sons of acting parents, who almost literally had the boards in his blood. Jim met him for the first time on *The Crowd Roars* in which he plays the best pal who is incinerated on the track due to Greer's ruthless driving in a needle race. Their long real-life friendship was a

The first of three boxing films, *Winner Takes All* (1932).

37

much happier affair. They made no less than ten films together between 1932 and 1941 and, with Pat O'Brien, formed the hard core of Hollywood's famous 'Irish Mafia'.

Winner Takes All, the first of three Cagney boxing films, came next, and is memorable only because Jim draws on his youthful streetfighting experience to pull all his own punches with stirring conviction. Using his nimble footwork learned on the New York stage and his fisticuffs acquired in gutter brawls, he trained long and hard to reach a professional level. His sparring partner was Harvey Parry, an ex-welterweight champion, and during their practice bouts, Jim lost fifteen pounds. As there was no dubbing in those days, the sound was recorded live and he paid particular attention to the noise made by leather on flesh so that that too was exactly authentic.

This meticulous preparation wasn't enough to salvage Roy del Ruth's film artistically though it did well enough at the box office. Cagney's broken-down prize fighter is hustled between an Arizona desert haven where he can recuperate from the blows inflicted on him by life and better boxers, and lowdown rings in unprepossessing parts of assorted towns. He never finds his true milieu on this switchback and his ladies, Marian Nixon and Virginia Bruce, are insufficiently talented to make the relationships work.

When *Winner Takes All* was finished, Cagney walked again. This time he demanded 4,000 dollars a week, the same as Edward G. Robinson, Douglas Fairbanks Jr. and Kay Francis (though 2,000 less than top earners Dick Powell and Ruth Chatterton), the current stars of the Warner's stable. To make his demand stick, he headed his car back east and drove slowly — as he always did — toward the town where he was born. On the way he chatted to reporters about giving up the cinema, going on a vaudeville tour of Europe, becoming a painter or a doctor. 'I don't care if I never act again,' he insisted, when the studio reminded him petulantly that he was under contract. 'There seems to be a curious legend that an actor can care about nothing but acting but if I never had to do another scene it would be all right with me. I have no trace of that ham-like theatrical yen to act all the time.'

True enough, but he was accustomed from his

Picture Snatcher (1933). **Left, as Danny Kean, gangster turned tabloid photographer, snatching more than pictures with Alice White, below. Overleaf, a little light hoofing with Ruby Keeler in** *Footlight Parade* (1933).

early youth to earning money in return for hard grind and he needed to go on doing so, mostly because he never quite believed his luck could last. Actors, he said, quite correctly, came and went, living high on the hog one month, flat broke and out forever the next. Then they had nothing left to do except listen to their arteries harden. Accordingly he never dared to split for real with Warner's, but continued to play his dangerous game.

The odds were stacked against him. The three Russian-Jewish brothers, who had gambled on the first talkie, *The Jazz Singer*, five years earlier in a last-gasp attempt to save their infant empire from bankruptcy, were now the most powerful force in the most hierarchical part of show business. And they were not about to back down before a ten-picture man, however much they'd profited from his fledgling career to date. In desperation, Cagney offered to make three pictures for them for nothing, in return for the cancellation of his five-year contract. No dice, said Jack Warner.

So, once again, the protagonists sat three thousand miles apart. Jim practised his dance steps or played tennis with Billie while letters poured into the studio taking his side and demanding they find a solution. Then came lawyers' letters, threats of legal action and, finally, due to the good offices of Frank Capra, a settlement. It only upped Jim's weekly pay packet by a hundred and fifty dollars from 1,600 to 1,750 so he may have wondered if it had all been worth it. However he went back to work and, as his next script was called *Hard To Handle*, it must be admitted that Warner's had the last laugh this time around.

Another monstrous hit, it featured Cagney as Lefty Morell, a con man who sees his chance in the Depression to play on human despair by organising a marathon dance contest and then a bogus treasure hunt. It develops into a classic case of the biter bit with the inevitable love interest and more than Cagney's normal quota of comedy. For once he seemed quite tolerant of the character he played, having amused himself by basing Lefty on a despised public relations man who had haunted his career. 'He never thought of anything but publicity,' he said of him. 'He used to make our lives a real burden. You'd see him jump up with a new idea. Next thing he was on a plane for San Francisco.' Lefty didn't go that far but he did organise a national grapefruit craze, a publicity-rich spin-off from *The Public Enemy* which gave the current crop of Warner's PR men a field day.

The second of the five films Jim churned out in 1933 was more in the old style of things, a comedy-drama called *Picture Snatcher* which set out to mollify the Hays Office's objections to overt sex and violence by setting the action inside a newspaper framework, a device also used for *The Front Page*, Cagney's Danny Kean is a partially reformed gangster who becomes a photographer for a gutter tabloid or, as his girlfriend puts it, 'the lowest thing on a newspaper, a picture snatcher. You steal pictures from folks who are so down in the mouth they can't fight back, just a thug doing the same thing you always did.'

This was the first of several Cagney-Lloyd Bacon collaborations and they usually worked well because Jim respected the director. 'He was a great guy to work with,' he recalled. 'On receiving a script, he wasn't one to say, When? Why? Where? How? He'd just way Who —, meaning 'Who have I got?'. Usually he got who he wanted — his gang, the stock company: Pat O'Brien, McHugh, Cagney, Allan Jenkins. It didn't matter what the hell the story was; when we went in to bat, we did the best we could.'

It's possible that *Picture Snatcher* was the fastest Cagney ever filmed. It took just fifteen days to wrap and Bacon was even printing rehearsal footage to bring it in on time. The Warner's schedules were another of Jim's perennial grouses and he complained — rightly — that there was never sufficient time to have a good script written and then develop the characters as he would have liked. It was the same on the next routine operation, *Mayor of Hell*, an intricate pseudo-reformist vehicle which has the star portraying a cut-price gangster who takes over the supervision of a boys' reformatory. His visionary plans, inspired by his girl, to let the inmates govern themselves meet with intial success but, after he goes off the rails, disaster becomes inevitable. There is an electrifying climax in which the golden rat-a-tat-tat Cagney tongue halts a brutal bout of juvenile mob rule that has already sent the autocratic warden to a grisly death.

Although the film received critical acclaim, Jim dismissed it as 'the old mixture as before, only more so'. 'Making pictures was a fatiguing business,' he explained, 'and I was kept plenty busy, and I mean literally to all hours. Frequently we worked to three or four in the morning. I'd look over and there'd be the director, Archie Mayo, sitting with his head thrown back. He was tired; we were all tired. This was the kind of pressure the studio put on us because they wanted to get the thing done as cheaply as possible. At times we started at nine in the morning and worked straight through to the next morning. We were completing in seventeen days, nineteen days, twenty-one days. Hell, we could have phoned them in.'

No doubt he would have preferred to in some instances but not for *Footlight Parade*, his long overdue debut as a singer-dancer and the role he cherished most from his early years in Holly-

With Margaret Lindsay in *Lady Killer* (1933).

wood. He plays Chester Kent, a naive producer who stages ornate theatrical prologues for cinemas. He is a law-abiding man and his job gives the perfect excuse for his portrayer to be seen composing original dance routines, trying them out himself, demonstrating them in rehearsal halls and even taking over the lead in the grand finale from a drunken star. Jim romps through it with obvious glee. Once again Lloyd Bacon sat in the collapsible canvas chair while Joan Blondell and Frank McHugh shared the boards, and there is the added bonus of co-director Busby Berkeley's choreography with all its frothy fantasy and gaudy splendour.

'He could learn whatever you gave him very quickly,' Berkeley once said in tribute to Jim. 'You could count on him to be prepared. And expert mimic that he was, he could pick up the most subtle inflections of movement. It made his work very exciting.' There could probably be no higher praise but the reviewer on 'Film Pictorial' tried hard. 'One of the surprises is Jimmy Cagney,' he proclaimed. 'Although he used to be a song and dance man in his stage days, he performs here in a manner that makes one wonder why his talent in this direction has not been used before.'

Jim, of course, wondered that for years, both before and after *Footlight Parade*, for smash hit though it was, it didn't set the scene for an immediate change of image. It is likely that it was a sop to the intransigent actor, an attempt to balance the books between gangsters and nice guys in order to keep him quiet. Anyway the pendulum swung back with a vengeance for *Lady Killer* which, as the title suggests, forced Jim to behave with more than his standard aggression towards yet another unfortunate dame. Once again it's grapefruit victim, Mae Clarke, who is ruthlessly dragged by her hair the whole length of a room before being hoisted bodily out of the apartment. This performance as a cinema usher turned con man turned screen idol is one that Cagney has always wanted to forget though audiences, titillated by seeing him bare to the waist in Indian guise, thought very differently.

Perhaps the most unexpected reaction to Jimmy's screen image was the way in which women themselves enjoyed his brutalisations of their sex. There he was, several inches short of six foot, red-haired and far from conventionally handsome. He certainly had a restless energy that could reasonably be promoted as sexual but he invariably described himself exactly as he was: a one-woman man. His priority was to spend time with Bill alone, rather than accompany her to Hollywood occasions. Female stars expected the drool treatment wherever they went but that didn't happen to the Cagneys. 'I never saw anyone fall off the top of a bus just because Mrs. Cagney crossed the street,' Jim once remarked, and both of them preferred it that way.

In fact Jim was chronically wary of strange women. He didn't, as many sympathetic letters addressed to Billie suggested, rant and rave around the house. In the privacy of his home in Hillcrest Road, Beverly Hills, that aggressive rapid fire speech became ultra quiet and he was embarrassed, not to say infuriated, by suggestions, frequently made by total strangers, that he used his wife as a punching bag. Yet he received a constant stream of requests from women asking, not that he should to to bed with them (as many stars did) but that he should grind half grapefruits in their faces!

In order to avoid such unwelcome and absurd attentions, he preferred small dinners in the homes of chosen friends, Blondell, McHugh, O'Brien and co, at which Hollywood politics soon gave way to a little hoofing and a lot of dirty Irish jokes. Hardly the ultimate in orgies but very much the Cagneys' way. This was also the time the 'Boys' Club' was founded. Its members were the Irish Mafia, as Hollywood called them, Jim, O'Brien, McHugh, Spencer Tracy and Ralph Bellamy. They, and other acceptable fellas, would meet every Thursday, invariably Jim's evening out away from Bill, for dinner in Romanof's or Chasen's or the Beverly Wilshire. There they ate well, chatted and laughed together. Each took his turn to pick up the tab and to reserve the table. Typically Jim would always ask for a corner one or, better still, a private room, so as to eliminate the staring eyes and pointing fingers of the gossip brigade.

1934 began as Warner's planned it should go on, with the first of four Cagney films. *Jimmy the Gent,* which marks his initial association with that skilled Hungarian-born director, Michael Curtiz, who would later make some of his very best films, notably *Angels With Dirty Faces* and *Yankee Doodle Dandy.* This frivolous comedy falls some way short of those triumphs, with Cagney taking the title role of Corrigan, a frenzied business agent who hunts up missing heirs to large fortunes for a living — and occasionally invents them in order to claim the money if they don't show up on command. Its curiosity value lies in its teaming of Jim with Bette Davis, the first time the pair appeared together. She plays a blonde secretary with the look of someone who wishes she was elsewhere — as indeed she did, for she was due to join the career-enhancing *Of Human Bondage* for another studio as soon as the picture was in the can. Nevertheless her philosophy that if a thing is worth doing, it's worth doing well appealed to Jim and they struck up a durable acquaintance that was strengthened by Bette's conviction that he was right about studio exploitation.

Jim's follow-up, *He Was Her Man,* was his last and with the possible exception of *Blonde Crazy,* his best joint-venture with Joan Blondell, an unrequited love story in which Jim is the gangster trying to escape vengeful rivals to Joan's tart with a heart. Yet, as soon as that good partnership ended, he struck up another, with Pat O'Brien in *Here Comes the Navy,* the first of a trio of service pictures they made together. Indeed the instinctive liking the two had for each other is the best thing about this simple sea-faring slugfest.

On its own, the film did little for either's career but by setting the pattern for the eight-film association, by far the most rewarding buddy-buddy relationship in Jim's career, it certainly broke new ground. O'Brien is the hard-headed senior officer to Cagney's rebellious salt, a juxtaposition between a serious God-fearing man and a devil-may-care adventurer that was to culminate four years later with the priest and the killer in *Angels with Dirty Faces.*

Just as there was a dichotomy between Cagney's roughing up of his screen women and his gentle treatment of his beloved wife, so there was a paradox between his screen and real-life relationship with Pat O'Brien. Where Jimmy was a dour campaigner whose customary nervy speedy performances could turn him into a whirling dervish of emotion and frenzy, O'Brien was an optimist whose rather lumpen features branded him as the ultimate in screen sinceres. Where Jim thought his career would fall in on him tomorrow. Pat was sure that the good times would last forever. Where Cagney described himself as an 'eight-and-a-half-hour a night man', O'Brien thought nothing of talking and boozing till dawn. then turning up without sleep on set for the next day's stint.

It was O'Brien who christened Jim 'The Far-Away Fella' by which he meant not only that he couldn't make his pal like the cocktail party circuit he loved so well himself, but that he was a thinking man who genuinely knew he had better ways to spend his time, whether he was down on the farm, at sea in a boat or out in the countryside: no matter which so long as he was as far away as possible from the Hollywood gadabouts.

Cagney, in his turn, recognised their differences. 'Pat definitely isn't a far-away fella, and he's remarkable in more than one way,' he wrote of his friend. 'He has, for instance more durability than anyone I've ever known. He would arrive on the set in the morning, having been up all night — clear-eyed, knowing all his words — and step cheerfully in front of the cameras. At day's end, home, have dinner; then he and Eloise would go out and again stay up all night. He had the cheeriest kind of upbeat optimism and he'd never accept my cautious attitude about Hollywood — that house built of cards, as I considered it. I'd say, 'Pat, stop and take stock,' but he'd never listen. He was for the jokes, the laughter, the nightclubs. The wonderful payoff is it didn't disagree with him in the slightest. He's still going strong in his eighties and he looks wonderfully well.'

Despite the O'Brien bonus, Cagney's year had a dismal finish with one of his worst films ever, a silly comedy called the *St Louis Kid*, remembered only for the role reversal that had the leading lady, Patricia Ellis, threatening him with a knife. The other point of note was that Jim, as a feisty truck driver on the St Louis to Chicago milk run, attempted to ring the changes by punching with his head rather than his hands. The producer was not amused. Nor, in any real sense was Cagney though he did feel he was making the best of a lousy job.

A better deal for Mae Clark from the *Lady Killer.*

It was about this time that Cagney joined The Screen Actors' Guild during the early months of its existence. With his track record, it seemed like a good idea to line himself up with his fellow actors to fight for better conditions. Once again the moguls, among the most anti-Union group in a notoriously anti-Union nation, were outraged, and did their utmost to divide and rule their employees by arousing suspicion one of another. This ploy was unsuccessful and the Guild grew to play an effective role, initially by introducing a much-needed eight hour day.

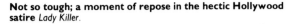

Jim's satisfaction was immense. 'What most moviegoers of the time didn't realise,' he remembered, 'was that actors as a group got less than two cents out of every dollar taken in at the box-office. Many actors were lucky to earn sixty-six dollars for a six-day week and they were forced to work almost every Saturday night. Getting off for a national holiday during the week meant they would have to work the following Sunday without pay to make up for that holiday. The actor was not only the low man on the totem pole, he was practically buried in the ground. I felt it was part of the producers' overall plan: keep actors poor so they can't argue about anything. But we did, and we won!'

That victory had rather more damaging consequences than he'd imagined when, in August 1934, his membership of the Guild, and particularly an article he'd written for its magazine, was held against him in a Sacramento Court which was trying to pin charges of Communism on him. Cagney's political bias has moved, like Ronald Reagan's, from socialism in the twenties to conservatism in old age, a progression he looks on as natural. In the mid-Thirties, though, he was a Rooseveltian Democrat, a stance disliked by certain fellow actors, among them John Wayne.

What made him more vulnerable, as far as the court was concerned, was that he was a soft touch. Not only had he given money towards an ambulance for the Spanish Republican Army, but he had made a contribution to the wife of his old friend, the muckraking Communist journalist Lincoln Steffens, to help the destitute Mexican cotton workers who were then dying of starvation in the San Joaquim Valley. He had never been a secret Party Member, merely a victim, fifteen years before McCarthy, of a witch-hunting policeman, Detective Ray Kunz, who was determined to find reds under the most unlikely beds. The Sacramento District Attorney, Neil McAllister, was of the same persuasion.

Back in Beverly Hills, a shocked Cagney made his own reply to these distant unsavoury courtroom allegations. 'I'm proud to call myself one hundred percent American,' he announced. 'This old country of ours has been pretty good to me. I started with nothing, worked hard and am today very comfortable. I believe that nowhere else is there the same golden opportunity for anyone willing to work hard as in America. I'm against all -isms except Americanism.'

McAllister never made his charges stick but the slur remained on the Cagney name, especially in Hollywood where tongues wagged remorselessly and the pathological hatred of Communism that would fuel McCarthy's fires was already established. Warner's clearly believed their star's innocence however for they would certainly have baulked at employing someone who had been dubbed politically unreliable.

Instead they gave him five pictures for 1935.

CHAPTER 4
TOP DOG

By the mid-Thirties, Jim was no longer on the up and up. He'd arrived. He was among the top ten players in box-office popularity, something he found essentially meaningless but which put him in a position of considerable power as he was to discover on his next walk out. Meanwhile he reported for duty on *G-Men*, directed by William Keighley, the first gangster picture in which he was allowed to perform on the right side of the tracks. His character, Brick Davis, is a decent lawyer who becomes a special agent, with licence to kill of course, when one of his buddies is gunned down in the street. From there on in it's Cagney against the mobs, the tough loner against the forces of evil.

The film was pivotal in Jim's career, proving he could play non-criminals in hoodlum pictures. The driving, determined Davis may be a million miles away from the reality of Gentleman Jim but he is equally far removed from the compulsively destructive Tom Powers. The actor himself admits that it was a step up the ladder artistically and recalls that it was the first film on which he protested about being shot at with live bullets. But he let it happen anyway — and fortunately survived.

By camparison his second film with Pat O'Brien, Lloyd Bacon's *The Irish In Us,* was a lot of harmless fun. It oozed Irish sentimentality with Cagney, O'Brien and Frank McHugh cast as the three rumbustious O'Hara's, respectively a ne'er do well, a policeman and a fireman. They have a pampering mother (Mary Gordon) and a girl (Olivia de Havilland), they'd all love to love which results in some good, clean, implausible argy bargy.

A Midsummer Night's Dream, Warner's improbable essay into high culture, was a de luxe production that garnered three technical Academy Award nominations without inspiring the critics or the public. Opinions differ as to whether it was a beneficial change or, more popularly, a brief aberration for Jim. In an all star cast that included Joe E. Brown, Olivia de Havilland, Dick Powell, Hugh Herbert, Frank McHugh and the young Mickey Rooney, he played Bottom. It was the only non-American part he ever played in a Warner's film (and one of very few in all his long career) but he contrived to

Cagney and George Raft are pleased to help the authorities in any way they can, in *Each Dawn I Die.*

48

A Midsummer Night's Dream **(1935). Top, a pat from Bottom for Joe E. Brown's Flute, Cagney's Shakespearean debut. Below, a further faery scene.**

turn Shakespeare's obstinate dullard into a bombastic home-grown version. As a confirmed ad-libber, he remembers the picture mostly because, with the Bard in the writing seat, such improvisations were forbidden.

The debate goes on as to whether *A Midsummer Night's Dream*, as directed by the German Max Reinhardt with plodding Teutonic concern for the spirit of its creator's imagery, was an honourable failure or a caricature of Europe's Shakespearean traditions. Either way, Cagney didn't much care. 'As Bottom, I simply had

another job to do, and I did it,' he said, 'There was no feeling at the time that we were doing anything special and I think the whole enterprise was a box-office disaster, although I believe the picture has taken on an aura of culture since then.'

Reinhardt, who had spent a lot of Warner's money and had a wonderful time, could afford to be more generous — and was, when he commented, 'For me, James Cagney is the greatest of the talkie stars. His acting gives a mysterious, dangerous terrifying uncertainty that never allows the tenseness of an audience to relax. His reactions are unexpected, fresh and never conventional. The part of Bottom has never been played with such uncanny artistry. The range of his genius is limitless . . .'

With his ass's swivel head barely removed, it was on to *Frisco Kid*, again for Lloyd Bacon, a boozing, gambling romp set in the less respectable parts of San Franciso in the Gay Nineties. Cagney's Bat Morgan is a high-living Barbary Coast sailor who makes a fortune in the Gold Rush but is set on the path of virtue by a female managing editor (Margaret Lindsay) just in time to escape the destruction meted out to his ex-partners by a vigilante mob. Cagney is back to his stirring, resistant self, both on and off the screen, when he comments sourly, '*Frisco Kid* was one of those catch-as-catch-can affairs put out solely because it had to be put out. By that I mean that the film had already been sold to the exhibitors before even a foot of it had been shot or conceived. This will give you some idea of its inherent artistic flavour. The picture was built just the way a Ford sedan might have been.'

Warner's should have taken note of the newly rising tide of ire but they didn't. Instead they pushed their recalcitrant star into Howard Hawks's *Ceiling Zero*. The part of Dizzy Davis, a flamboyant flier who flirted with death delivering mail in thick fog — the Ceiling Zero of the title — was rather better than most, as was the film, due to the film maker's skill and the presence of O'Brien alongside Cagney. But it was the fifth film of the year and his contract specified four: he walked, he filed suit against Warner's — and this time he didn't return for two years.

The battle was to be long and hard, in studios, newspapers and courts. Batting for Jim was his brother Bill, who had arrived in Hollywood in 1931, tried acting himself, then gradually taken over as his brother's business agent. He was a tougher nut to crack and, largely through his determination not to see Jimmy fleeced, the fight continued through many more rounds than its predecessors. Jim was certainly in a dilemma and

once again he retreated to the east, this time to Martha's Vineyard where he had achieved his lifelong dream of buying a farm. From time to time, he issued his familiar war cries: he would join the Abbey Players in Dublin (they denied it); he would form a group of players recruited from the 'Boys' Club' — O'Brien, McHugh, Bellamy — to take J. M. Synge's 'Playboy of the Western World' on the road.

Overtures from Hollywood were made as well. Wealthy producers, among them Sam Goldwyn, David O. Selznick and Darryl Zanuck, now the power behind the throne at Twentieth Century, were keen to put Cagney under lucrative contract, but only if Warner Brothers gave the go-ahead. This they resolutely refused to do, seeing Jim's stand as the thin end of a wedge that could be driven right through the star system that had served them so well. The other studios watched nervously, pleased in a way at a rival's discomfiture but apprehensive as to the wind of change the rebellion might herald in their own corridors of power. Most of the stars, and especially the gutsy Bette Davis, looked on with equally keen interest and Warner's were right in thinking that some of them were planning for it to be their turn next, if Jim came out ahead.

When the courts found for Cagney by declaring that ten films was one too many for 1934-5, Warner's promptly appealed against the decision and the combat continued. Jim stayed east, sailing his yacht Martha in the waters off Cape Cod, tilling the soil, learning to ride a horse and renovating the 200-year-old farmouse. The neighbours were wary at first. What was this real tough gangster man doing in their peaceful isolated community? But they warmed to the couple when they saw Jim's true nature and, in the way that islanders have, they were ferociously protective of his privacy, so far as outsiders were concerned, once they understood his antipathy towards intruders. That suited Jim just fine.

After a year of argument had ended in stalemate, Cagney signed up with the small, newly formed but poverty-stricken independent, Grand National Pictures, where he was a huge fish in a tiny pool. He would get 120,000 dollars per picture and the right to select his own material. It was goodbye, for the time being, to 'girl-hitting micks'. Instead he became an amiable meat inspector, one Johnny Cave, in *Great Guy*, a title picked to reflect both Cave and Cagney. Cave is for the little man, a crusader for the Bureau of Weights and Measures who fights the cheats who defraud shoppers on grocery weights. Mae Clarke, repaid at last by Jim for the grapefruit incident, co-stars and the balance is set right by having her dominate the relationship and win every argument.

Cagney sat in on every story conference and it

As Bet Morgan in *Frisco Kid* (1935). Overleaf, as Dizzy Davis in *Ceiling Zero* (1935).

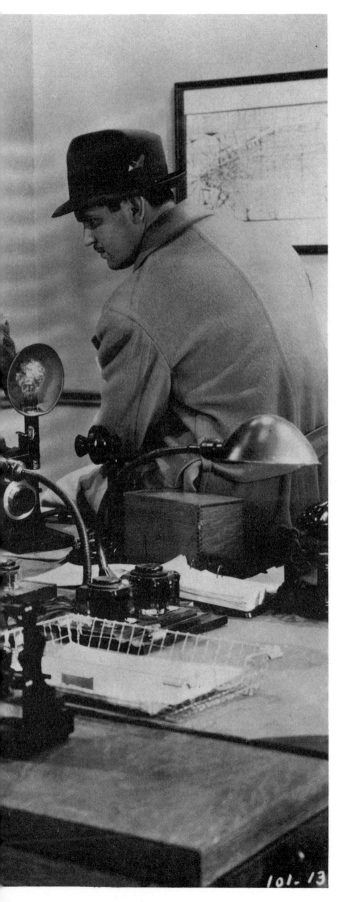

shows in the hero's decent homespun values, his dislike of violence, even though he occasionally succumbs to it, and his indefatigably caring approach to his work and his life. The film exposes corruption in big business and politics without glorifying it, reflecting Cagney's own beliefs. And it worked, as the reviewer for the 'New York Times' was quick to note. 'The entire movie,' he wrote, 'bears unmistakable evidence of that Hollywood rarity, complete co-operation of the director, the story and the casting departments.'

For the second Grand National film, *Something to Sing About*, Jim allowed himself the luxury of becoming a hoofer again. It is clearly autobiographical, and a personal crack at the studio system to boot. The hero, Terry Rooney, is a New York band leader who sets out for Hollywood and stardom. He gets his contract and finds himself billed as the acting sensation of the day, despite his protests that he is a song and dance man at heart. When he explodes during the shooting of his first film and storms off the set on his honeymoon cruise, the cameras keep turning so that he comes back to find that his 'tough guy' image has stuck. The ensuing debacle threatens to ruin his marriage but, following the course of true love, he eventually abandons his career and returns to New York.

The plot is blatantly sentimental and the sets were threadbare due to Grand National's characteristically faded fortunes but Jim made his point, as one British film critic recognised when he wrote, 'The film shows us an entirely new James Cagney, one we have never seen before, a band leader, a song and dance man, a film star who guys the Hollywood routine with all the flair of a born comedian and a born dancer who seems to out-do Fred Astaire at his own game. There is no one in Europe with such snap, such speed, such skill who at the same time is capable of attuning these gifts to the triumphs of social principle.'

It is not certain that Grand National could have afforded to stay in business with or without their star but they were spared the humiliation of saying so for the Appeal went Warner's way, leaving Cagney with the choice of toeing the line or leaving the cinema altogether. In the event, through the good offices of Pat O'Brien, the 'professional againster' as Jack Warner called him, came to terms with the studio. Although he would earn a princely 150,000 dollars a picture, Jim was once again a Warner's man.

If he'd thought his protests about the quality of the scripts he'd be offered would change anything, he must have known he was in for a disappointment when he read the one for his

Left, the shopper's crusader in *Great Guy* (1936).

comeback film, *Boy Meets Girl*. It lays strong claims to be his flimsiest comedy ever. Lloyd Bacon directed and Cagney shares the limelight with O'Brien, the pair of them playing Hollywood screenwriters who turn a baby into a movie star. The performances are speedy but, given such totally inadequate dialogue, the end product is reduced to an insignificant farce. As a satire about the movie business, *Something to Sing About* had the legs on it any day.

Nor did his complaints about typecasting seem to have made any impression on the studio when his next project came up. Once more he was to be a gangster, a tough guy on the short slide towards the electric chair but this time, Warner's were right to insist. The part was Rocky Sullivan; the film, the superb *Angels With Dirty Faces*, directed by Michael Curtiz.

This is surely the high point in the screen relationship between O'Brien and Cagney, the picture in which their friendship away from work produces the perfect synthesis of their talents. At the start, Rocky and Jerry Connelly (O'Brien) are slum kids lifting a few insignificant items from a stationary railroad car. When they are disturbed, Jerry has the faster sprint and it is Rocky who is caught and condemned to spend his youth in various penal institutions. Jerry grows up to become the neighbourhood priest and, when Rocky is released, he begs him to go straight. Instead he finds himself idolised by a gang of street kids and involved in a minor hoods' war with Humphrey Bogart's shyster lawyer. The murder and death sentence that follow merely enhance Rocky's local reputation and it is left to Jerry to demand the ultimate sacrifice from his cocksure pal, that he should turn 'yellow' on his way to the chair so that his young supporters will lose faith in him — and, more important, stop imitating his life of crime.

The scene in which he accedes to his friend's demand is brilliantly handled in silhouette with Jim crying out and writhing in a frenzied anguish of terror against the restraining arms of his captors. Ever since, as he explained most recently to TV chat-show host Michael Parkinson when he appeared on his programme to publicise *Ragtime*, people have been coming up and asking him if he really turned yellow or merely simulated it for the father, to which he invariably replies, 'I think in looking at the film it's virtually impossible to tell which course Rocky took — which is just the way I wanted it. I played it with deliberate ambiguity so that the spectator can take his choice. It seems to me it works out fine in either case. You have to decide for yourself.'

The picture is the first of three Cagney-Bogart

Left, the happy hoofer in *Something to Sing About* (1937). Overleaf, putting one over on Bogart in *Angels With Dirty Faces* (1938) . . .

associations, with Jim very much ahead of the game at this stage. Bogart is mean and glowering, then fearful as he faces death at Rocky's hands, but his part is strictly supporting. O'Brien is another matter and this is undoubtedly one of his very best career performances. Cagney may look on the film as just another 'cuff opera' in which he improved an insubstantial script by improvisations along the way but he builds a magnificent characterisation which has been imitated by stand-up comics around the clubs ever since.

With every sharp movement, precise gesture and rat-a-tat-tat delivery, Rocky Sullivan becomes a living breathing human hoodlum. Jim based it all on a man he knew when he was a kid, as he revealed in his autobiography: 'He was a hophead and a pimp with four girls in his string. He worked out of a Hungarian Rathskeller on First Avenue between Seventy-seven and Seventy-eight Streets — a tall dude with an expensive straw hat and an electric blue suit. All day long he would stand on that corner, hitch up his trousers, twist his neck and move his necktie, lift his shoulders, snap his fingers, then bring his hands together in a soft smack. His invariable greeting was "Whadda ya hear? Whadda ya say?" The capacity for observation is something every actor must have to some degree, so I recalled this fella and his mannerisms and gave them to Rocky Sullivan just to bring some modicum of difference to this roughneck. I did that gesturing maybe six times in the picture — that was over thirty years ago — and the impressionists are still doing me doing him.'

Jim's gift for imitation won him the New York Critics' Award as Best Actor, an Academy Award nomination and, what for him was undoubtedly more important, first place in the earnings league for 1938 with 234,000 dollars in the kitty. Now he was really being treated like a star, pampered and pandered to on set and off it. He was as ever totally professional in his approach to his work, on time, meticulously prepared and word perfect. In return he expected to complete the shooting promptly and be on the next train East to Martha's Vineyard. The studio also had to accept that his publicity exercises would be strictly at his discretion which meant very rare indeed. As a result the time between pictures was very much his own which was just the way he wanted it.

Early 1939 found him back under Lloyd Bacon's direction for his first western, *The Oklahoma Kid*, which he claims was mangled by Warner's beyond recall. He'd had his own plans for his character, the redoubtable outlaw of the title, and they included a worn shirt and pants. These were hurriedly replaced by a winsome white suit and a stetson which, as co-star Bogart remarked, made Cagney look like a 'mushroom under a huge western hat'. In constrasting black,

59

representing evil to Jim's good, Bogie shared the action as the leader of the desperadoes, and once again he ended up dead.

Jim did his own riding and even some of his own roping — of which he was inordinately proud — but the clichéd plot was bound to finish up as a fancy love story decked out in western trappings. 'There's something entirely disarming about the way Cagney tackled horse opera,' wrote Frank Nugent for 'The New York Times', 'not pretending for a minute to be anything but New York's own Jimmy Cagney, all dressed up for a dude ranch. He cheerfully prances through every outrageous assignment his scriptwriters and directors have given him.'

One suspects that, as far as Jim was concerned, George Raft was the best thing about his next project, *Each Dawn I Die.* For this he returns to journalism as a muckraker whose belief in the machinery of justice is rudely shattered when he is framed for manslaughter by a crooked lawyer whose activities he has exposed. Raft's hardened lifer is already inside and much murder and mayhem occur before justice can be seen to be done. The film is tightly directed by William Keighley and the Cagney-Raft pairing is inspired with Raft's composure the perfect foil for Jim's volatile, impassioned presence.

. . . but, left, proving to Ann Sheridan that he's not all bad. Below, was he yellow or wasn't he? On the way to the electric chair.

In Raoul Walsh's *The Roaring Twenties,* Jim winds up the decade in style as Eddie Barlett, a gallant First World War soldier who returns to New York to find that all job doors are closed to him and that the girl he's been writing to from the trenches is still at school. Dispirited, he becomes unwittingly involved in bootlegging, then more willingly in the purveying of bathtub booze. It's classic get-rich-quick stuff as he stalks the speakeasies in white tie and tails, the epitome of vulgar elegance. His main rival for top dog is his fellow victim of the trenches, George Hally (Bogart) and it is he who finally wins out after the Black Tuesday of the Stock Market crash on Wall Street in October 1929.

Poor susceptible Irish Eddie, left with one cab by his rival with which to earn a living and having already lost his girl (Priscilla Lane) to a rum-runner turned lawyer, stops drinking milk, as he always has done, and embraces gut rot alcohol.

Cagney is at his balletic best in the memorable final death scene when he zigzags through the streets, then pitches down the steps in front of a huge church to lie sprawled and motionless in front of the one real friend he had. 'He used to be a big shot,' she says to an anonymous passing cop, a fitting epitaph from one pal to another. Jim also profits from the variations of this part, impeccably suave when he's up, a down-and-out lush when the tide turns. In this his third and final appearance with Bogart, he is competing with him for acting honours, but maintains his edge due, at

Above and right, deadly rivalry with Bogie, both on and off the set of *The Roaring Twenties* . . . but he finds a real chum in Gladys George, top.

IT'S A STAR-BIG
PARADE OF GLORY!

JAMES
CAGNEY
PAT
O'BRIEN
DENNIS
MORGAN

"THE FI

with GEOR

hting "69"th

Directed by

JEFFREY LYNN   WILLIAM KEIGHLE
ENT · ALAN HALE · DICK FORAN

Original Screen Play by Norman Reilly Raine, Fred Niblo, Jr. and Dean Franklin

least in part, to having the rounder role to play. Bogie's dour determination followed by his 'yellow' act when death by gunshot becomes inevitable, are familiar from *Angels With Dirty Faces*, but he performs with more depth here and the qualities that will shortly make him *the* tough guy of the Forties are beginning to show.

'Mr. Cagney, of the bull-calf brow, is as always a superb and witty actor. Mr. Bogart is, of course, magnificent,' was how Graham Greene summed it all up. But Jim himself, although his gangster is redeemed in advance by being the victim of a society which doesn't care for the patriots who were prepared to die for it, never rated the film very highly, though he might have thought differently had he realised Eddie was to be his last hood for ten years.

He recalled long hard hours on the set knocking shape into what he described as 'the silly thing'. It was a way of working he'd become accustomed to over the years. Hollywood writers, briefed to churn out material to order at high speed, rarely achieved either sparkle or originality so it was up to the actors, assisted by the director, to re-structure the bland story lines and execrable dialogue into something rather more worthwhile. It wasn't unusual for several participants to make suggestions before shooting the one the majority thought best.

The new decade opened with two Cagney-O'Brien features, the last films they would make together for forty years. *The Fighting 69th*, an astutely timed tribute to the heroic deeds performed by that great New York Irish regiment in World War I, was a natural for Warner's stock of Micks. Cagney is cast as a cowardly braggart who causes his comrades' death due to insubordination, only to be persuaded to redeem himself

through personal gallantry by O'Brien's army chaplain. Backing up the principals were Frank McHugh, George Brent, Tommy Dugan and Alan Hale. The film, which was described in the New York Times as 'a middling war picture with all its obvious theatrics, hokum and unoriginality,' was a smash hit, especially after one of Cagney's infrequent publicity appearances on its behalf at Grand Central Station in front of 5,000 fans.

No one had much to be proud of in *Torrid Zone*, an absurd jungle romp made on Warner's thirty-one-acre back lot in forty-one days. Cagney is a horse-riding trouble shooter, O'Brien a cigar-puffing banana baron and the lovely Ann Sheridan, also from *Angels with Dirty Faces*, a card-sharping hitch-hiker who matches them line for line. The film is memorable, if at all, because Jim wears a narrow moustache, grown he says in a desperate attempt to give his character a third dimension. When it was revealed to the Warner's top brass, their howls of protest could be heard on the other side of town. The fringe was thought to be toughness-reducing and they could never stand for that. In the end, though, they had to, for the star stayed stubborn and the moustache stayed in place.

City for Conquest was an altogether more sophisticated affair, based on a novel by Aben Kandal which Jim found things to admire in. Accordingly he went back to work with rare enthusiasm and dieted down from 180 lbs. to 145 lbs. in order to be in shape for the fights, which, as always, he insisted on doing himself. Cagney's Danny Kenny is a New Yorker, who punches well enough to turn professional but is perfectly content to drive his truck until his ambitious girlfriend (Ann Sheridan) insists he go into the ring. There he turns out to be red hot, winning fight after fight, until an unscrupulous opponent throws chemical in his eyes and grinds it in with his fists, so blinding him for life.

The rest is pure goo. Kenny's brother, a hack songwriter who would rather compose symphonies, eventually does exactly that and dedicates one of them to the blinded hero, reduced by this time to selling newspapers from a corner street stall in New York. As it plays on the radio, his erstwhile girl walks by . . .

There seems to have been some friction between Jim and the director, Anatole Litvak who told 'Films and Filming', 'Only once in my life did I have any difficulty and this was with Jimmy Cagney. He couldn't quite adjust to the part and I came to an impasse with him'. Others have laid the blame for the film's unevenness on Litvak himself but Jim is not among them. The best

The Fighting 69th, **as the cowardly soldier turned hero in the First World War.**

footage, he insists, was left on the cutting room floor.

'I worked like a dog on the film,' he explained. 'There were some excellent passages in Kandel's novel, passages with genuinely poetic flavour, and all of us doing the picture realised that retaining them (as we were doing) would give *City for Conquest* distinction. Then I saw the final cut and this was quite a surprise. The studio had edited out the best scenes, excellent stuff, leaving only the novel's skeleton. What remained was a trite melodrama. When I realised what they'd done, I said to hell with it and that cured me of seeing my pictures thenceforth. I even wrote a letter of apology to the author.'

In *Strawberry Blonde*, based on the Broadway play 'One Sunday Afternoon', Jim takes a walk down memory lane to turn-of-the-century Manhattan, only to find a very different place to the one where he was born. For this tragi-comedy of long-lost love is set against a background of merry horseshoe-throwing contests and meetings between young couples in moonlit parks. Biff Grimes (Cagney) is a dentist who has learnt his trade from a correspondence course, then left it to work for a con man he loathes (Jack Carson) because he has married the strawberry blonde (Rita Hayworth) of Biff's innocent youthful desires. Even when he lands up in prison, having been made the fall guy for his rival's business frauds, he can't forget her, and that despite the fact that he has a far nicer wife (Olivia de Havilland) waiting loyally for him outside.

Raoul Walsh's picture, which has an unusually good script and a neat twist at the end, is one of Jim's very best comedies. That he thought so too is proved by his having it re-titled in honour of his mother. Carolyn had been a strawberry blonde herself and there was a family legend that, when she was sixteen, she'd been to a dance with a man called Eddie Casey. As they swept around the floor to the hit tune of the moment, 'Casey would waltz with the Strawberry Blonde,' they were the cynosure of all eyes. Carolyn, now sixty-three, was on the set when her son, with Rita Hayworth in his arms, re-created her night of triumph nearly half a century before. And so another slice of Cagney history was made.

By this time Jim and Billie had been joined in Los Angeles by all the family. Both Harry and Eddie had set up medical practices. Carolyn lived with Eddie, preferring his more down to earth business neighbourhood to the rarified heights of Coldwater Canyon and Beverly Hills where Jim and his brother Bill were established. In 1941 Jim and Billie had further cause for happiness when they adopted two children, James Cagney Junior and a girl they christened Casey. As sister Jeanne

With Ann Sheridan in *City for Conquest* **(1941).**

James CAGN
Ann SHERIDA

CITY FOR CONQUEST

was also making her mark in the film industry, the Cagney clan was well and truly set up in the Californian sunshine. Despite Jim's wealth and fame, the brothers still maintained their four-against-the-world attitudes, enjoying nothing so much as each other's company for an evening of song and dance and inside jokes.

Meanwhile Warner's showed no signs of putting their errant hoofer back on the boards. Instead they teamed him with Bette Davis for *The Bride Came C.O.D.*, another comedy but one which fell far short of its potential due to being directed for farce by William Keighley. Cagney is a charter flyer who is offered ten dollars per pound weight by a Texan oil tycoon if he can return his spoiled daughter (Davis) before she marries an obnoxious band leader (Jack Carson). Naturally the couple, after a lot of love-and-loathe sequences, fall in love while stranded in the desert. Ms Davis, who was clearly unenthusiastic about the abortive project both before and afterwards, had this to say in her autobiography. 'It was called a comedy. It had been decided that my work as a tragedian should be temporarily halted for a change of pace. Jimmy, who had made the gangster artistic — Jimmy, who was one

of the fine actors on my or any other lot — Jimmy, with whom I'd always wanted to work in something fine, spent most of his time in the picture removing cactus quills from my behind. This was supposedly hilarious. We romped about the desert and I kept falling into the cactus. We both reached bottom with this one.'

Maybe, though, there are those who found *Captain of the Clouds*, Jim's first film in colour, even worse, despite being directed by Michael Curtiz. It was a cash-in on war fever, a propaganda exercise which has Jim playing an American backwoods pilot who volunteers for the Royal Canadian Air Force in time for the Second World War, there after many conflicts with authority, to die a hero in the fight against fascism.

And so, Jim must have felt, it had to be. More bad scripts, bad films, bad vibrations. More money, more hits, more time with his family. Those were the losses and profits of his life and career in 1942. He'd made thirty-eight films in thirteen years, immortalised the gangster in only a handful of them but the tough guy in almost all. He badly needed a change, an artistic success, a break from the grinding routine. He thought about volunteering for the war. Instead he went to see an obscure film called *The Phantom President*. Its star was George M. Cohan and the visit to the cinema was to change his life.

With Rita Hayworth, Olivia de Havilland and Jack Carson in *The Strawberry Blonde* **(1941).**

Right, as a charter flyer in pursuit of Bette Davis' spoiled heiress in *The Bride Came C.O.D.* **(1941).**

CHAPTER 5
ONCE A SONG AND DANCE MAN...

By 1942 America had undergone a radical change of mood. From the moment bombs dropped on Pearl Harbour the preceding December, the country had stopped trying to keep out of what it had seen as someone else's war and buckled down to battle, sending thousands of servicemen around the world to fight the good fight against fascism. At home support for the war effort boomed and, with public morale in mind, Hollywood was enlisted to make pictures that showed America as worth fighting for, worth losing a son for, worth dying for.

Many of these were truly dire, mere propaganda exercises in which god-like WASPs tangled with hideously vicious Japanese in cliched bellicose situations. Others, like *Casablanca,* profited from the complexities and excitements of espionage in far-away places. But only one waved the flag with such unremitting vigor that it swept all before it in an incredible rising tide of patriotism, and that was *Yankee Doodle Dandy.* And the main ingredient in its triumphant progress was the brilliant, volatile performance of James Cagney in the film that finally made him happy.

Like Jim, George M. Cohan was an Irish American, a New Yorker, a hoofer and a family man. His stage was Broadway for which he wrote forty-four shows, all but two of them comedies, and over 500 songs. He appeared in many of them in person, raised the money to keep the ball rolling and earned himself a reputation, in many places, of being the greatest American light entertainer of the early twentieth century.

By this stage, he was old, ill of the cancer that would kill him late in 1942 and forgotten, with just one show left to sell — the story of his life. He wanted it to be filmed with style and taste. Some time before he had approached Sam Goldwyn who offered it to his resident song-and-dance man, Fred Astaire, who turned it down. Next on the list was Paramount who refused to come up with the goods as Cohan envisaged them. The project got a bit further at MGM but, once again,

Stepping out, in *Yankee Doodle Dandy.*

74

Cohan's insistence on final control earned the thumbs down. Not only was he known to be a stubborn adversary with an Irish temper and a capacity for digging himself in but his hatred of Hollywood and all it represented was legendary, so none of the moguls was keen to take a chance on him. Next came the proposition that Mickey Rooney should play Cohan while George portrayed his own father, a device that would have allowed him to keep his finger permanently on the pulse, but that too evaporated.

Meanwhile Bill Cagney, in his managerial role, was looking for a property to restore his brother's tarnished reputation. The Communist slur, started by the Sacramento affair in 1935, had never really gone away. Indeed two years earlier, when merely hoping that Hitler would be defeated smacked of pinkoism in some West Coast quarters, Jim's name had appeared on a list of alleged heavy subscribers to the Party assembled, for reasons that remained forever obscure, by former Los Angeles Communist supremo, John R. Leech. That he shared the list with Bogart, Franchot Tone, Clifford Odetts and Frederick March among others was little consolation for Jim as it made the resulting glare of publicity all the more ferocious.

Once again the news came rather late to Cagney. He was on holiday in Massachusetts at the time and he had to break his rule — and his pact with Billie — of never flying so as to reach San Francisco in time to defend himself in front of Representative Martin Dies and his House Un-American Activities Committee. Even the power-hungry Dies was unable to sustain the charges when the actors had given evidence and had to dismiss them, but the scars and the doubts in the public mind remained.

So when Bill heard of the possibility of a musical biography of George M. Cohan, he pursued it, initially without telling his brother. When Cohan had checked up on Jim through a mutual friend — apparently he didn't remember his forthright rejection of the fledgling vaudevillian in 1926 — he gave the go-ahead for Cagney to play him. Then the project was presented to Jack Warner, a script that was sufficiently flattering to Cohan was duly prepared and passed by him, in return for which he agreed to sell Warner Brothers the right to base the film on his life for 100,000 dollars.

It was only at this stage that Jim got to know about the affair. Being as keen as Bill to exorcise the Red Scare, he was delighted, until he read the script which he pronounced dull, humourless and unworkable. Once again the project was nearly

'George M. Cohan' going through his paces with his 'wife', Joan Leslie in *Yankee Doodle Dandy* (1942).

wiped out. Warner's, fearing the reactions of both Cagney and Cohan, didn't know which way to jump and it was left to Bill and Jeanne Cagney, who'd been cast as Cohan's sister, to put the pressure on. Anyway all that singing and dancing were mighty tempting, so Jim was eventually persuaded to sign, provided the script was revamped by the Epstein brothers, Julius and Phil, who'd injected a bit of much-needed adrenalin into some of his past pictures.

Intensive rehearsals followed. Under the watchful eye of Johnny Boyle, who had played in The Cohan Revue of 1916 and so had first-hand knowledge of the entertainer's style, Jim conquered his individualistic stiff-legged technique and the run up the side of the proscenium arch he'd invented and made so very much his own. Jim's legs stood up to it and in due course he was as ready as he'd ever be, though he claims the workload was so intensive that the numbers were never quite second nature to him, as he would have liked. Johnny Boyle was less fortunate, injuring one of his feet so badly that he virtually never danced again.

If there were any shortcomings in the magnetic Cagney footwork, they were noticeable to him alone. His old mentor, Michael Curtiz, directed and there was a feeling of incipient success, of being in the right place at the right time, about the shooting that inspired the performers. That versatile talented actor, Walter Huston, is compulsive as Cohan's father while, on the distaff

side, Rosemary de Camp and Joan Leslie, as his mother and wife respectively, are excellent.

Even so it is Jim's film. He is electrifying throughout, a whirlwind figure whether he's singing 'I'm a Yankee Doodle Boy', dancing down the stairs of the White House after receiving his Congressional Medal of Honour (the first ever presented to an entertainer) from President Roosevelt, matching steps with his fellow Cohans in the family act that made him famous or proposing to his wife in one of the cinema's best, understated love scenes. His factional Cohan is undoubtedly a much nicer guy than the arrogant and disputatious George M ever was while the jingoistic, flag-waving patriotism is more than a little dubious forty years on, but nothing can diminish Cagney's spellbinding triumph. He sang, he danced, he acted as he never had before — and the crowds cheered him to the echo.

Once they got to see him, that is, for it wasn't until the 1,500,000 dollar film was in the can that Warner's faced up to the fact that the script was quite different to the one originally approved by Cohan and that he still had the power to veto it. By this time, he was too ill to come to the West Coast. Instead he enlisted the services of Ed Raftrey, then President of United Artists, and asked him to vet the finished article. It was only when the tough 300 lb. Irishman broke down in tears at the end of the screening that Jack Warner

Another angle on *Yankee Doodle Dandy.*

The moment of triumph: Gary Cooper presents the Best
Actor's Oscar for *Yankee Doodle Dandy*

and Bill Cagney could breathe again. Cohan too saw the picture before he died and pronounced himself well satisfied with his memorial, much to Jim's relief. 'I like to think that this only contact we had was professionally appropriate,' he said: 'one song-and-dance man saluting another, the greatest of our calling.'

When the time came for *Yankee Doodle Dandy* to open in Los Angeles and New York, it was decided that the tickets to the premiere should be free provided would-be members of the audience bought War Bonds, valued from 25 to 25,000 dollars each. On the West Coast, the first to fork out the maximum was Al Jolson and in all nearly 6 million dollars were raised, enough to buy three Liberty ships for the North Atlantic convoy run. The same system was adopted in London, with War Savings Certificates costing £5 to £5,000 on sale, and nearly a million pounds were raised.

Both critics and audiences were ecstatic. 'The magic of *Yankee Doodle Dandy* is conjured up by the consummate Cagney portrayal,' wrote the 'New York Herald Tribune's' Howard Barnes. 'He even looks like Cohan at the time and he has the great man's routines down cold. The point is that he adds his own individual reflections to the part, as should certainly be done in any dramatic impersonation of a celebrated figure. He has given many memorable and varied screen performances in the past, but this is nothing short of a brilliant tour-de-force of make-believe.' London's 'Daily Mirror' had this to say: 'Just seen a great new musical comedy star. In its way it's the biggest discovery of the war. The name? James Cagney. Yes, I mean it. In *Yankee Doodle Dandy,* this lady-socking tough guy dances and sings like Fred Astaire and puts up his best acting performance to date.'

When the Academy Award season came around, the film got eight nominations, including the best picture, director, original story, supporting actor (Huston) and actor (Cagney) but Jim was the only winner in any of these major categories. When Gary Cooper read out his name, the applause brought the house down, which was appropriate because it was to be his only Oscar, and that for his most satisfying performance, as he later recognised in his autobiography.

'*Yankee Doodle Dandy* turned out to be something I could take real pride in,' he wrote. 'Its story abounds in all the elements necessary for a good piece of entertainment. It has solid laughs, deep warmth, great music. And how much more meaningful are those patriotic songs today in view of our current national troubles! *Yankee Doodle Dandy* has lots of reasons to be my favourite picture. When I got the Academy Award that year, I was able to say my few acceptance words with some feeling: "I've always maintained that in this business you are only as good as the other fellow thinks you are. It's nice to know that you people thought I did a good job. And don't forget it was a good part too. Thank you very much." Praise from your peers generates a special kind of warmth.'

Legend has it that he gave the Oscar to Bill the next day as a gesture of thanks for his part in the affair. Be that as it may, the Cagneys were to see a lot more of each other from now on for Jim, cashing in on his rocketing reputation, decided to end his love-hate relationship with Warner's for ever and set up his own production company to make the kind of pictures he'd always wanted. To Jack Warner, it must have seemed the final irony to lose his star just when he'd let him hoof his way to immortality but Bill Cagney, writing in the 'New York Times', had a different perspective.

'After some unimportant parts, what happens?' he asked. 'Jimmy gets the lead in *The Public Enemy.* You see how it works out. Suddenly Jimmy clicks as a strictly "dese, dem and dose" guy. A tough mug, so tough that every gangster in the country was nuts about him. Jimmy was made but that wasn't all. He was typed — typed as exactly the kind of guy our mother had tried to push us farthest away from. So for ten years, he makes five pictures a year to the Warner Brothers formula. He is a heel for eight reels, then clean him up in the ninth. You didn't like it, you argue, you're suspended, you get a reputation as a difficult actor — so you usually give in.'

But not this time, for Jim's contract had expired and he had the biggest hit of his career on his hands which made raising the finance (from The Bankers Trust of New York and Security First National of Los Angeles) to set up Cagney Productions pretty simple. In addition, having earned 362,500 dollars in 1941, 5,000 more than runner up in the earnings league, Clark Gable, and that before *Yankee Doodle Dandy,* he had more than enough groceries on the table to last him and his family for the rest of their lives. So the time had come to take a chance and make himself an artist. Accordingly Bill Cagney became president of the fledgling company and Eddie its business manager. United Artists promised to distribute the finished products. All that was needed were the scripts from which to deliver the goods.

The first vehicle was *Johnny Come Lately,* a whimsical exercise in nostalgia featuring an ageless heroic artist-poet-tramp called Tom Richards. He has no background, no roots and no purpose unless it is to exude love of humanity as he follows his hobo trail across America. Typically, with Cagney in the driving seat, the environment is rural with Richards arriving in a small town, there to be spotted by an elderly newspaper woman, Vinne McLeod, as he sits reading The

A restraining hand from Grace George in *Johnny Come Lately* (1943).

Pickwick Papers under the statue in the main square. Intrigued by this, she rescues him from a vagrancy sentence and enlists him in her journalistic battle against corruption.

The stamp of Cagney is clear for all to see. His tramp, who has been described as Chaplinesque, is sensitive, kindly and charming, resorting to violence only to protect his patroness against a death threat. He rejects the young love interest in favour of fascinating flirtatious exchanges with mature women. And his cartoons for Vinne's newspaper, sketched in with bold, confident strokes, cause an upsurge in circulation which may save the editor from imminent ruin. Clearly, Richards, like Cagney, is one of nature's gentlemen, a loner more at home choosing his own destiny on the open road than hemmed in by regular work and other people's demands.

The acting also sets a standard and a philosophy for Cagney productions. The splendid Broadway actress Grace George is exceptionally good as Vinnie McLeod in her only film role and she is backed up by what 'Time' magazine recognised as one of the best troupes of supporting actors ever assembled. 'Bit players who have tried creditably for years to walk in shoes that pinched them,' they wrote, 'show themselves in this picture as the very competent actors they always were. There has seldom been as good a cinematic gallery of U.S. small-town types.'

That kind of praise meant something to Jim, the current president of the Screen Actors Guild and a performer who was notoriously supportive of lesser-known members of his peer group. Indeed he had been accused by Jack Warner on more than one occasion of delaying work in progress so as to gain further days on the set for bit part players and extras. Although it is unlikely, given his formidable professionalism, that the hold-ups were anything but genuine such an action would have been very much in character.

As far as *Johnny Come Lately* was concerned, it was fortunate that the praise for the casting pleased him; it was all he was to get. Opinions differ nowadays as to whether the film was a Capra-esque masterpiece (albeit directed by William K. Howard) or a sentimental cop-out but, at the time, it was a financial and critical disaster. John T. McManus summed up the consensus opinion, '*Johnny Come Lately* is almost the kind of business that might result if Jimmy Cagney, the immortal Hollywood star, had returned to play the lead in the annual production of his old high school's Masque and Film Club. It is so palpably amateurish in production and direction, so hopelessly stagey, uneven and teamless in performance and so utterly pointless that it is bound to cause raised eyebrows wherever it is shown.' To which Archer Winston of the 'New York Post' added, 'To put it bluntly it's an old-fashioned story told in a very old-fashioned way. Please, Mr. Cagney, for the benefit of the public, yourself and Warner's go back where you made pictures like *Yankee Doodle Dandy*.'

No way, said Jim, although *Johnny Come Lately*'s flop meant he couldn't raise the money for the second Cagney production until 1945 — and even when he did, he may well have wished he hadn't. *Blood on the Sun,* made in the last year of the war, is a blatant cash-in both on Cagney's tough-guy image that was supposed to put bums on seats and on the anti-Japanese sentiment that was rife in America following Hitler's defeat.

Once again Jim plays a crusading journalist, this time on assignment in Tokyo in the Twenties where he exposes a plot by the tinpot fascist Tanaka to take over China and rule the East. Jim, having prepared with his customary thoroughness through the good offices of a Japanese-American instructor he'd rescued from the detainment centre in which he'd been interned during the war, did his own judo, though he nearly broke his neck in the process. Less commendably, he

slapped his female lead, Sylvia Sidney, on the face in the grand old Cagney way. That she claimed to enjoy it is no excuse for the man who had ranted so long and so loudly against the image of broad-hitting mick and it is hard to avoid the conclusion that Cagney was more than a little hypocritical. What was unacceptable if Warner's forced it on him was apparently quite okay if expediency — and his own company — demanded it.

Not that it did him much good for *Blood in the Sun* was so mediocre in script, direction and performance, that it sank without trace. At the time this second failure had the edge taken off it by a much greater blow, the death of his beloved mother, the victim of a series of strokes that partially paralysed her before the end. 'Mom died when she was sixty-seven,' he said, in final tribute, 'and there was hardly a day of those years that had not been spent in giving.'

In an attempt to revitalise his fortunes, Jim signed up with 20th Century-Fox for *13 Rue Madeleine* in which he plays Bob Sharkey, a wartime spy who gives his life behind enemy lines on a desperate intelligence-gathering mission against the Germans. He made 300,000 dollars for eight weeks work but not much else because the film was a mere time filler, the part a standard Warner's tough guy, albeit without criminal connections. Still the cash was useful, especially as he had a much cherished project in mind, a film version of William Saroyan's Pulitzer prize winning play, *The Time of Your Life*, to be screened as written.

The wild-eyed, idiosyncratic and apparently humourless playwright had already turned down several lucrative offers for his hot property but, after discussion with Jim, he agreed to sell him the film rights for seven years. Brother Bill set to work to assemble a *Johnny Come Lately* type cast that would do justice to the strange tales told by the group of bizarre people gathered together for the duration in a San Francisco waterfront bar. Among them sits Joe (Cagney), another happy-go-lucky rootless charmer who philosophises while he puts back bottle after bottle of Mumm champagne. He is wealthy and unpredictable, a compulsive gambler and fantasiser.

Most unusually for the highly mobile Cagney, he is a stationary character who refuses to dance, saying, 'I don't even like to walk.' This gives a new dimension to Jim's acting for he contrives, while remaining seated until the final brawl, to use his voice and eyes and mouth — he compulsively chews gum throughout — to build his portrait of the inquisitive, rather intellectual but always amiable Joe.

The play was filmed very much as written, but with the important difference that Jim re-made the ending after audience previews so that no one dies. Instead the Cagney fists are called into play to give the bar's resident bully a proper hiding, a less violent climax certainly but one which casts further doubt on the star's determination to quit fighting for good. Brother Bill was again successful in assembling a formidable cast which included his sister Jeanne as a melancholy ex-hooker, the

The bar-room philosopher in *The Time of Your Life* **(1948).**

83

ex-vaudevillian James Barton as the pathological liar and William Bendix as the bar's owner. Add Broderick Crawford, Ward Bond, Paul Draper and James Lydon and you have quite a picture. William Saroyan thought so too when he wrote to Cagney Productions.

'Early one morning,' he said, 'I stood in line and bought a ticket for the first showing of *The Time of Your Life* in San Fancisco. I did this because as you know, I wrote the play and I wanted to find out as quickly as possible if my kind of writing could be made to mean anything at all in a movie. The people came into the theatre and sat down and finally the lights dimmed and the movie started. It wasn't more than three minutes until I had forgotten I had written the play. I was too busy enjoying it to care who wrote it. All by way of telling you I think you have made one of the most original and entertaining movies I have seen.' Far from claiming any share of the credit for himself, he went on to add that the film makers had translated 'a most difficult and almost unmanageable body of material' into the cinematic medium with considerable skill.

But most of the critics and the public proved that if they couldn't have the James Cagney they knew and loved, they were quite prepared to do without him altogether. An exception was James Agee who hit the nail on the head with his words in 'Time': 'Those who made the picture have given it something very sure. It's obvious they love the play and their work in it, and their affection and enjoyment are highly contagious.'

Cagney Productions lost half-a-million dollars on the film, some of it because the director H. C. 'Hank' Potter and his cameraman spent two weeks on pure rehearsal, blocking out the whole production, only to change their minds as soon as the cameras started turning and some of it because United Artists' distribution was totally inadequate and the box-office returns were dire. Clearly independence wasn't suiting Jim too well. By 1946 his earnings had dropped to a third of their 1941 level, he was approaching fifty and the new disaster heralded worse to come. Drastic steps were needed if things weren't to deteriorate completely and, in the event, Cagney did the most cataclysmic thing he could have done: he returned to the Warner's fold, so fulfilling the prophecy his old adversary, Jack Warner, had made several years before: 'He'll find out he needs me as much as I need him.'

What's more he agreed to play his toughest hoodlum yet in the gruesome blockbuster, *White Heat.* Bill may have secured a more realistic partnership with the studio by which they split the

Desperate intelligence gatherer behind enemy lines in *13 Rue Madeleine* **(1946).**

profits with Jim right down the middle but there is no disguising the fact that the psychopathic Cody Jarrett made Tom Powers look like a fun-loving adolescent. Nevertheless the role is one of Jim's finest achievements, marking as it does the transition from the young Cagney to the mature persona in one of the great post-war gangster films.

What is stranger still is that there is little doubt that Jim himself developed the vicious dementia of Cody Jarrett, with the assistance of that excellent director, Raoul Walsh. In one sense the wheel had turned full circle and he was back where he started in *The Public Enemy* — with a mother, his last as he was getting a bit old for them, a gun and a girl (Virginia Mayo) to kick around. Only this time the mother (Margaret Wycherly), far from having Ma Powers' lovable homebody innocence, was as brutal as her son, a domineering, twisted inhuman being with affection for nobody except her oddball offspring. Cody is tied to her coat tails as if by the umbilical cord, a clinging child-like madman whose searing headaches only she can cure. 'It's like having a red-hot buzz saw inside my head,' he cries in torment, and her hands effortlessly soothe away the pain. The scene in which he hears of her death while serving his prison sentence is one of the most celebrated displays of blind incapable violence in the cinema. Nor does Jim blow it, as he so easily might have done by letting rip immediately. Instead there is a moment of private grief, head in hands, followed by the charge through the vast dining room of a mortally wounded bull.

As for the gun, Cody uses it with the casual indifference of a kid with a pea shooter. From the first killing, when he blasts a train engineer during a heist, through the notorious hot dog sequence in which he chews unconcernedly while machine gunning a stooge through the boot of a car to the climactic suicide on top of a huge gas tank, he never shows the slightest concern about death. As he pumps the self-destructive bullets down between his feet, he laughs hysterically in final proof of insanity, crying out above the blaze of white heat that envelops him, 'Made it, Ma. Top of the world!'

Much of the plot and even more of the detail of the character came from Jim's famous memory. It was he who suggested that Cody Jarrett should be a psychotic in order to account for his actions, that he should have those terrible headaches and even that he should sit in his mother's lap, a throwback to a scene in his first movie *Sinner's Holiday* when Harry Delano did just that. 'Let's see if we can get away with it,' he said to Walsh — and they did. For Cody's madness, he drew on a childhood visit to a school friend's uncle in a hospital for the insane on Ward's Island. 'My

God, what an education,' he recalled. 'The shrieks, the screams of those people under restraint! I remembered those cries, saw that they fitted, and I called on my memory to do as required. There was no need to psych up. You don't forget that kind of thing.' Clearly, from his portrayal of Cody Jarrett, he hadn't.

Although, from mid-1949, the *White Heat* funds poured in, the film raised widespread doubts as to its social acceptability. Bosley Crowther in the 'New York Times' praised Jim when he wrote, 'Mr. Cagney plays it with such dynamic arrogance, such beautiful laying out of

White Heat (1949), with Edmond O'Brien and Virginia Mayo.

detail that gives the whole picture a high charge,' but added: '*White Heat* is a cruelly vicious film and its impact upon the emotions of the unstable or impressionable is incalculable. That is an observation which might be borne in mind by those who would exercise caution in supporting such matter upon the screen.' The 'Cue' reviewer agreed: 'In *White Heat*,' he wrote, 'you are subjected to an unending procession of what is probably the most gruesome aggregation of brutalities ever presented on the motion picture screen under the guise of entertainment.'

In its way, however, *White Heat* was as revitalising a force in Cagney's career as *The Public Enemy* had been. It was the first gangster picture to break the social consciousness mould. Cody didn't have a poverty-stricken childhood or an alcoholic father to excuse his behaviour: he was just mad. The changing morals of the post-war era allowed this greater licence; technical advances did the rest. A new type of hoodlum was born. And a new type of Cagney, greying, paunchy for the first time, tougher than his forerunners. This was his face for the Fifties.

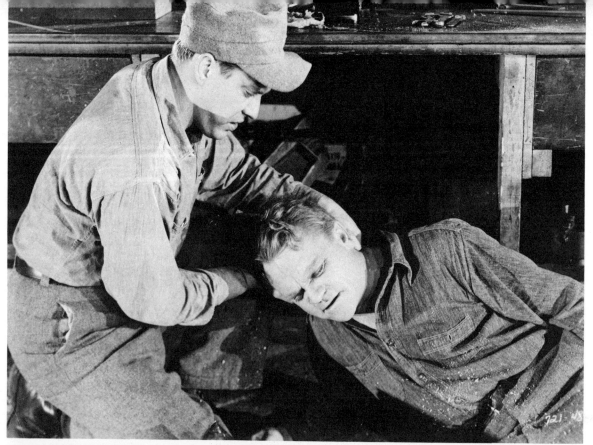

White Heat. **Top, Edmond O'Brien massages away the pain. Bottom, locked away with Robert Osterloh, Edmond O'Brien, and G. Pat Collins. Right, 'Made it Ma. Top of the world.'**

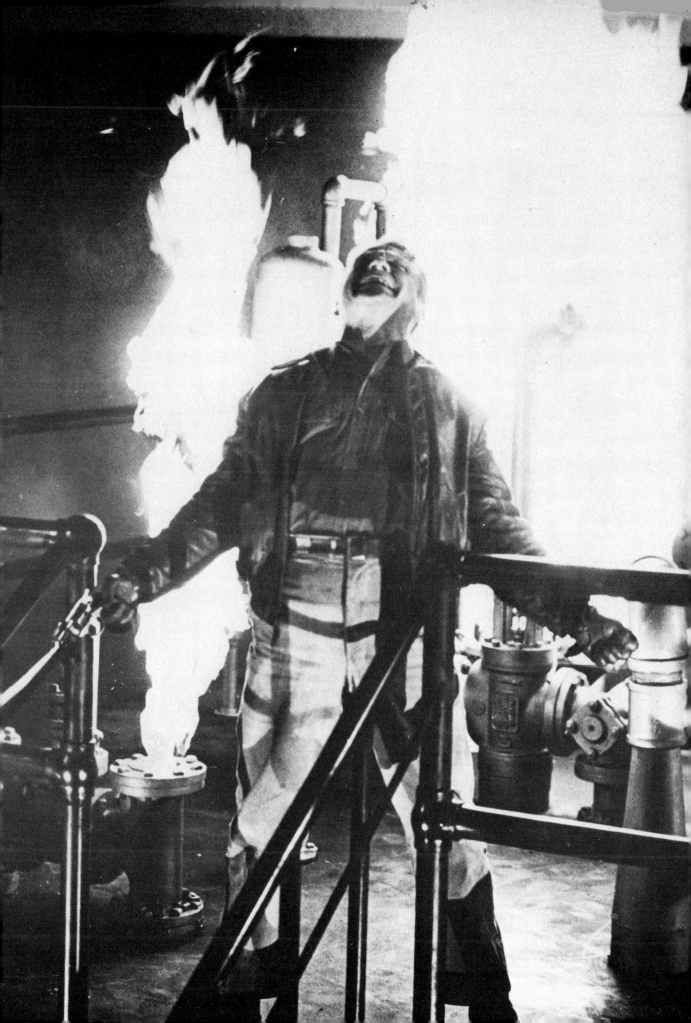

CHAPTER 6
INDIAN SUMMER

Over the next decade Jim made eighteen films, a production rate more in line with the contract Thirties than the more selective Forties. In the nature of things, some were good, some bad and some indifferent, but it is noticeable that the Cagney spark rarely blazed as it had done. It's not that he wasn't as professional, as prepared and as ready with his suggestions as ever but there is an ominous feeling that his heart was no longer in it. Effectively, the system had beaten him.

From now on, he would work for anyone who would hire him without expecting miracles. If a script, a cast or a director seemed promising, fair enough, but Jim knew, from bitter experience, that the best footage was as likely to end up on the cutting room floor as in the can. Unless, of course, Cagney Productions made the films and that, after *The Time Of Your Life,* wasn't financially possible on a regular basis. He certainly hadn't struggled long and hard to make himself one of the richest actors in the business in order to squander it all on principle and pictures no one wanted to see. Groceries, as always, came first.

One reason he was able to stop bucking the system was that his youthful idealism had all gone out of the window. By 1950 the man who'd been a soft touch for the workers in the San Joaquim Valley and the Republicans in Spain had swung so far to the right that he was in absolutely no danger from McCarthy's red-under-the-bed purges that were then sweeping Hollywood. His shift in perspective had begun during the heady patriotic days of the mid-Forties when the war was being won and *Yankee Doodle Dandy* was raking it in all the way to the bank. Then Roosevelt died and was succeeded by Truman. From being a Rooseveltian Democrat, Jim became a Dewey Republican, a move in which he was joined by Ronald Reagan. It put him in the same camp as his longtime adversary on matters of principle, John Wayne, and he has remained there ever since. It also alienated him from his old and considerably more consistent friend, Spencer Tracy, who had started out in the centre and remained there while Jim careered from left to right of him.

Spence was disgusted with what he felt was a cynical shift, ascribing it to Jim's immense wealth.

As Admiral 'Bull' Halsey, World War Two hero, in *The Gallant Hours* **(1960).**

90

371-63

There was a direct link, he observed, between the Cagney riches and his increasingly right wing and politically intolerant stance. 'No actor has a right to be *that* rich,' he remarked, meaning so loaded that he was no longer concerned with his fellow men.

Not surprisingly, Jim himself didn't see it quite that way but more as an obvious change of heart for a middle-aged man faced with new generations who didn't share his values. 'I believe in my bones,' he said, 'that my going from the liberal stance to the conservative was a totally natural reaction once I began to see the undisciplined elements in our country stimulating a breakdown of our system.' He had no doubts as to where the blame lay for his country's predicament and slated the liberals freely for their laxness in the schools and for letting the nation's youth do exactly as it pleased. From his new point of view, anything that smacked of wishy-washy liberalism was out and stern authoritarianism ruled okay.

Ironically Jim's fortune finally brought him in line with the studios he'd fought for so long. He now had the power to veto anything but, as if the battle for the right to say no had been the only thing that mattered, he rarely used it. Like the moguls, he protected his own interests and if that meant films that exploited the lowest common denominator, then so be it. At last the bosses and the ghetto boy turned tycoon could be seen to understand each other though the writing had been on the wall for some time. The young idealistic Jim would never have hit a girl under the Cagney Productions banner as he did in *Blood On The Sun*; nor would he have gone back to Warner Brothers for the socially dubious *White Heat*. From now on in, he would move with calm detachment towards the day when he would no longer have to work at all.

In keeping with this, his first Fifties picture was *West Point Story*, designed by Warner's to relate to *Yankee Doodle Dandy* in much the same way *White Heat* related to *The Public Enemy*. To Jim, that meant song and dance which was just fine, and squeezing into a West Point cadet's uniform which clearly wasn't. He did it anyway, having first prepared himself by visiting the military academy to check out the way the boys there lived. As neither the Lower East Side nor Hollywood had turned up many officer cadets, he was stranded for once with no personal experience to draw on so it was a necessary precaution. As a result of his researches, he turned in a splendid performance as Bixby, an out-of-work punch-happy Broadway musical director who is persuaded to stage the annual West Point variety show . . . and, in the grand olde showbiz way, to

Pointing the finger of the vicious paranoiac, Ralph Cotter, in
Kiss Tomorrow Goodbye **(1950).**

take over the lead at the last minute for the grand finale, after he's accidentally knocked out the most nimble-footed of the cadets.

Sadly the soppy story and the by now unfashionable patriotism, as directed by Roy Del Ruth, dragged the whole affair down to the depths. 'If everything about *West Point Story* were anywhere near as good as Jimmy Cagney is in it,' wrote the indefatigable Bosley Crowther, 'this would be the top musical of the year. The measure of his impact on the whole tenuous show is patently indicated when he is not on the screen. For then the thing sags in woeful fashion, the romance becomes absurd and the patriotic chest-thumping becomes so much chorus boy parade.'

Under the *White Heat* deal with Warner's, there was still a little life left in Cagney Productions which enabled the company to make *Kiss Tomorrow Goodbye* in 1950. One of the conditions of what was essentially a co-production was that the studio would give the first 500,000 dollars the picture made to the banks to wipe out the money Cagney Productions still owed on *The Time Of Your Life*. *Kiss Tomorrow Goodbye*, adapted from a steamy novel by Horace McCoy, is another gangster film featuring a vicious paranoiac. It has been hailed by the likes of Paul Schrader and Raymond Durgnat as classic film noir ('dark, pessimitic, corrupt and relentlessly cynical', said Durgnat) but others, among them the author of 'Cagney: The Actor as Auteur', Patrick McGilligan, see it as Cagney's antidote to *White Heat*.

'While *White Heat* is a violent, uncompromising movie,' he wrote, 'that brilliantly exploits every dirty angle of criminal degeneracy, *Kiss Tomorrow Goodbye* is really an ethical, moral, socially principled work that trickily reverses the major premises of *White Heat* into an exposé and condemnation of unbridled gangsterism. The major figures of both films are homicidal paranoiacs and the main situation of both stories concerns a jailbreak and then a "big job". There the similarities end, for Cagney is the hero (however unconventional — nevertheless, the sympathy-tinged protagonist) of *White Heat* and the villain of *Kiss Tomorrow Goodbye*.'

This villain, Ralph Cotter (Cagney), is a big-shot gangster and proud of it. He thoroughly enjoys engineering a blood-soaked prison break-out and a brilliant blackmail and robbery scheme involving the cops. He is unremittingly evil throughout, murdering his pal during the escape from jail and whipping his leading lady (Barbara Payton) with a rolled-up bathroom towel. Unlike Cody Jarrett, who was merely mad, he is bad through and through. And he receives his just desserts, which is why the film can be seen as morally buoyant. Not only is he shot down in the street to die in pain and squalor (in marked contrast to Jarrett's splendidly dramatic suicide on top of the gas tanks) but he is condemned in court from beyond the grave by his own brother (played by Bill Cagney) as the unscrupulous and brutal criminal he was. A triumph for righteousness, law and order that was very much in tune with Jim's contemporary thinking.

Indeed the whole transformation of Cotter from McCoy's pages to Cagney's script was designed to blacken the character until he became a stock Hollywood baddie. In the book Cotter speaks in the first person, a device that has the effect of justifying his actions to the reader, whereas the film observes him with total objectivity. Again in the novel, his associates are as corrupt and immoral as he is. His girl is a tough gangster's moll, and unfaithful with it, while his buddies are uniformally rotten to the core. The cinema Cotter however has a fresh faced innocent for a girl, someone who will automatically draw audience sympathy when swatted with a towel.

McCoy's hoodlum is a many-faceted man. He is a university graduate with a Dillinger complex, a Southerner with connections with the church, a musician and dancer. In other words, a man of talent who, having murdered his grandmother when he was a child, has turned to crime for the compulsion of it rather than to make a dishonest living. It is not to Cagney's advantage as an actor that he strips most of this background away, dehumanising Cotter into a mere shadow of his literary self, but it certainly allows the film to sustain its high moral tone.

Much worse was to come in 1951 when Jim made two dire films *Come Fill Your Cup* and *Starlift*. The first, directed as was *Kiss Tomorrow Goodbye* by the unoriginal Gordon Douglas, is a soggy drama about a reformed alcoholic reporter

Time to laugh with Raymond Massey on the set of *Come Fill the Cup* **(1951).**

(Cagney) who fights a long battle for sobriety not only for himself but for several of his drunken fellow scribes, followed by a short battle for survival in a gangster codicil tacked bizarrely onto the end. The male sob story of a plot meanders gently through two hours of inconsistent clichés before exploding into its supremely improbable finale. Not even Cagney's measured portrayal of an ageing drunk teetering on the brink of yet another stupor (he based the performance on his friend, Jim Richardson, City Editor of the 'Los Angeles Examiner'), nor the excellent support he receives from Raymond Massey, Gig Young and James Gleason, can conceal its fundamental slightness.

In *Starlift,* a galaxy piece, Jim finally got to play himself playing George M. Cohan in a cameo among a bevy of stars. Anyone who was anyone at Warner's was conscripted for this disastrous compilation, among them Gary Cooper, Virginia Mayo, Doris Day and Gordon Macrae.

Nor was its intention particularly honourable, as 'Time' magazine explained. '*Starlift* was Hollywood's ill-starred project of ferrying troops of movie performers to Travis Air Force base to the north of San Francisco to entertain replacements bound for Korea and wounded veterans on their way back to U.S. hospitals. But the film of *Starlift* is guilty of the worst breach of good taste when it takes a low bow for Hollywood's patriotic gesture, makes the project seem exclusively Warner's and includes some stars who never troubled to fly to Travis Air Force Base.' The writer went on to explain that whereas the real *Starlift* project was meanly funded by the studios at just 5,000 dollars (which rapidly ran out causing it to be cancelled), the celluloid rip-off cost 1,000,000 dollars which would have been more decently spent on continuing the original scheme.

Nor did *What Price Glory?,* even as directed by John Ford, do anything for the flagging Cagney reputation. Originally Jim, ever a sucker for a little hoofing, had succumbed to the promise of a musical version, only to find, after he'd made his commitment, that Ford had scotched that idea. Instead Maxwell Anderson and Laurence Stalling's Twenties Broadway play was converted into a rough and ready — and mostly unfunny — Fifties comedy with a few songs tacked onto it at inappropriate moments. Dan Dailey plays Sergeant Quirt to Cagney's Captain Flagg in a series of rumbustious World War I encounters that don't add up to much.

The critics unkindly noted Jim's paunch, and even his acting took some unaccustomed flak. 'James Cagney and Dan Dailey,' wrote Alton Cook in the 'New York World-Telegram and Sun', 'have lowered their acting standards in keeping with the vehicle.'

In 1953, Cagney Productions made their last

With John Derek and Viveca Lindfors in *Run For Love.*

independent, *A Lion Is In The Streets,* once again in collaboration with Warner Bros. Jim plays Hank Martin, a southern shyster lawyer who turns politician. Having faked a reputation as a defender of share cropper's rights and made himself a front runner in a race for the governorship, he is eventually exposed as a fraud by his friends and his wife (Barbara Hale) and gunned down in the streets by a representative of the people he has systematically cheated. The character, based on the southern politico, Huey Long, had already been immortalised by Broderick Crawford in the Oscar-winning *All The King's Men* in 1949 and Cagney showed no signs

With his protege, played by John Derek, in Nicholas Ray's western, *Run For Cover* (1955).

of equalling, let alone surpassing him. Even his acting school southern accent slips into New Yorkese from time to time.

Once again this is very much a family affair, with Jeanne Cagney playing the people's assassin, Bill producing and Edward editing the story. Better perhaps that he hadn't, for his inexperience shows in a badly thought out, long winded and almost unwatchably irritating film. Raoul Walsh's direction is pretty wayward too and the only thing that can be said for the picture is that

Sheriff of all he surveys: *Run For Cover.*

the James Cagney message comes over loud and clear: those who err from the straight and narrow must be seen to be punished.

Once again the public didn't want to hear it and the short, unhappy and above all unprofitable life of Cagney Productions was at an end. What had begun a decade earlier with so much optimism had come to nothing. Neither the earlier films with their unworldly loner heroes, nor the later ones in which pure villainy got its just desserts had attracted critics or audiences so that was that.

At this point Jim took a farming break for close on two years, to return in 1955 with four releases. A comeback, trumpeted the industry, to which the star retorted, 'Comeback, hell. I've never been away.' He had great hopes for the first of the quartet, Nick Ray's western, *Run for Cover,* an example of the Fifties 'distrust' movie of which *High Noon* was the brand leader.

This sub-genre was inspired by McCarthyist paranoia and the Cold War. The characters were noticeably duplicitous, each concealing a dark past; they showed an illogical distrust of strangers that nevertheless turned out to be well founded; and they were prepared to band together on the

side of the angels, in other words the law. *Run for Cover* has all these establishing features with Cagney as Matt Dow, an ex-jailbird, albeit for a crime he hadn't committed, who is appointed sheriff of a small town. After a bank robbery in which his protege (the young John Derek, now rather more famous as the husband of Bo) is involved, Dow sets out alone to bring the villains to justice. As a final irony, he kills the boy he loves like a son just as he has rejoined the goodies by shooting one of the robbers.

Ray has always claimed that Dow, who is kindly towards his wife (Viveca Lindfors) and paternal towards the boy, is the closest Jim ever came to playing himself on film. 'We have always seen Cagney as the tough little squirt who's throwing grapefruit in a girl's face or taking on somebody twice his size and kicking hell out of him,' he said, 'but Jimmy has not only a great serenity such as I've not seen in an actor, outside Walter Huston at times, he has a great love of the earth, and of his fellow man, an understanding of loneliness. I wanted to try and use all that. The vehicle itself wasn't strong enough for it and we didn't have the time to be as inventive as we would have liked.'

Cagney agreed in spades about the shortcomings but put the blame for them elsewhere when he wrote: 'Run for Cover seemed to promise something deeper in content than the average western. We had tried to make it as offbeat as possible but whoever cut the film was evidently revolted by anything but clichés. As a consequence, little things that Nick Ray (a good man) and the actors put in to give the story extra dimension were excised very proficiently. The result was just another programmer.'

Much better was Love Me Or Leave Me, a gangster classic which earned Jim his third Oscar nomination for Best Actor, a lot of critical acclaim and a mightily revived reputation. Directed by Charles Vidor, it was an adaptation of the lives of a nightclub singer, Ruth Etting (Doris Day), her first husband, Martin 'The Gimp' Snyder (Cagney) and her accompanist-lover, Johnny Alderman (Cameron Mitchell). All these protagonists were still alive and kicking at the time but large payments from the MGM studio enabled their experiences to be filmed, warts and all, instead of prettified Hollywood-style, to avoid law suits.

And that, as far as The Gimp went, meant very nasty indeed. Snyder was a Chicago laundry racketeer who walked with a limp throughout his life as a result of a pre-natal polio attack. His mind was as twisted as his body and he was almost incapable of human emotion. Cagney's Gimp lives in a brutal and isolated world of his own in which he attempts to conceal his loneliness behind a facade of sarcasm and violence. For him, attack is the only means of defence.

As usual Jim had prepared well and had his answer ready when the real Gimp asked where he'd learnt to imitate his walk. 'I didn't,' said Cagney, 'I had observed people with that kind of affliction and I knew that doing the limp with any kind of support gadget would be intrusive. So what I did was very simple. I just slapped my foot down and turned it out while walking. That's all. Mr. Snyder liked the picture by all accounts.'

So, unusually, did Cagney who recalled his initial pleasure on reading the script. 'I thought, "My God, yes, we go with this one,"' he commented. 'There was nothing to be added, nothing to be taken away. It was in fact that extremely rare thing, the perfect script. I was so pleased to find one that didn't need any help, any devices. Among other things, I was pleased with the biographical honesty.'

He was also more than pleased with his leading lady, Doris Day, who he'd appeared with previously in West Point Story. This time, however, they were on equal terms and Jim recognised an exceptional talent. 'I saw something in her I hadn't noticed before,' he commented, 'or maybe it was just coming into bloom. I don't know. She had matured into a really exceptional actress. She had a beautiful basic simplicity stemming from a lack of guile. And that lack of guile photographs. That quality, coupled with genuine acting ability, is irresistible to an audience.'

Evidently the admiration was mutual for Doris replied in kind. 'He's simply the most professional actor I've ever known,' she said. 'He was always "real". I forgot we were making a picture. His eyes would actually fill up when we were working on a tender scene. And you never needed drops to make your eyes shine when Jimmy was on set.'

This highpoint of Jim's Indian summer also bore critical fruit. It was summed up by William K. Zinsser in the 'New York Herald Tribune'. 'Cagney,' he wrote, 'has created a fascinating portrait of The Gimp. In every mannerism — heavy limp, coarse speech, taunting sarcasm, flashes of rage — he moulds an obnoxious character who tramples over everybody in his lust for power. It is high tribute to Cagney that he makes this twisted man steadily interesting for two hours.'

Heady times indeed but then it was business as usual for Mister Roberts and The Seven Little Foys. The former, a lightweight comedy drama about a near-mutiny caused by an obstinate Captain (Cagney) on a naval ship in the Pacific, had several plusses from its star's point of view. One was a few weeks' swimming, interrupted by only minimal work with fellow performers Henry Fonda and Bill Powell; another was a second opportunity to work under John Ford, at least until ill health caused him to be replaced by Mervyn LeRoy. Best of all though was that he got to know Jack Lemmon, a rising talent he'd spotted and admired on television.

At their first meeting, Jim asked Jack, 'Tell me, just how left-handed are you?', at which the startled newcomer looked completely blank. Jim repeated the question but Lemmon was still baffled until Cagney explained he'd seen him playing a soda jerk on television during an hour-long play in a totally left-handed manner.

'Oh, I'm not left-handed at all,' Jack replied. 'As a matter of fact, I'm so right-handed that I decided to play everything left-handed and to make it a mark of the performance. Just for the challenge of the thing.' And so another mutual admiration pact was signed. Jim could only admire such a professional approach while Lemmon was amazed that the ever-observant Cagney had spotted a detail that his own wife had missed. They've been fast friends ever since. 'The overall experience of just being with that man was wonderful,' Lemmon observed several years later. I can't ever remember being with him for sixty seconds and finding it dull.'

Obviously *Mister Roberts* was a Warner's attempt to cash in — successfully as it turned out — on Bogart's triumph as Captain Queeg in *The Caine Mutiny,* one of the big timers of the year before. The character was a similar martinet, tyrannical and cranky, opposed by an assortment of lovable sailors with moral right on their side. *The Seven Little Foys,* which followed, was even less original, a biopic of vaudevillian Eddie Foy, George M. Cohan's lifelong rival and enemy. Jim resumed as Cohan in a cameo table-top routine opposite Bob Hope's Eddie Foy. He took no payment but rehearsed as doggedly as ever, not least because it was a splendid excuse to lose weight.

'The man is a horse,' Hope exclaimed in exhausted amazement after rehearsals. 'A work-horse. Here he was doing this thing free and working like a demon. Why he danced ten pounds of suet right off me. I'll bet he lost a good fifteen pounds himself.' He also nearly did his knees in for good. By the time he came down off the table-top, they were twice their normal size due to fluid build-up and the agony was intense. After a few weeks they went down but as Jim remarked, even for a song and dance man, fifty-six is not fifty.

Jim's third western, *Tribute to a Bad Man,* came his way by chance when Spencer Tracy's persistent complaints about the script and the locations forced his long-term employers, MGM, to discharge him in mid-picture. The call came through from studio chief, Nick Schenck, to Cagney at Martha's Vineyard where he was resting up after a busy year. He wasn't exactly over-joyed to answer it but go he did, tempted perhaps by the story of Jeremy Rodock, a hard line ranch owner whose proud boast it was that he could transform wild horses into beautifully trained animals.

Whether he was only there for the horses or not, he turned in an impeccable performance, making the tough Rodock, a man who habitually

With Henry Fonda in *Mr. Roberts.*

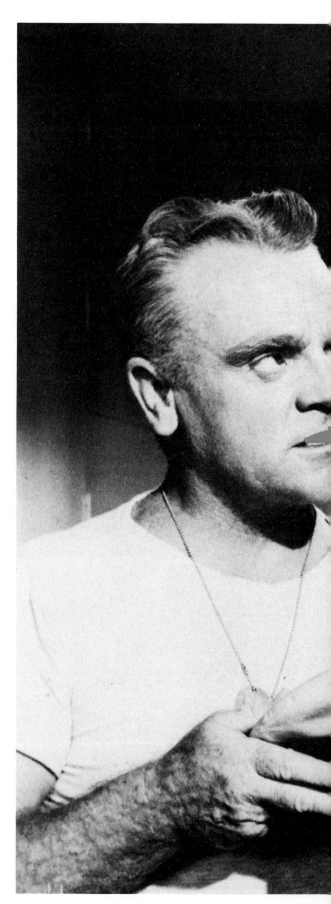

hangs cattle rustlers, into a three dimensional character by giving him a peaceful home life between such aggressions. Irene Papas, in her first Hollywood film, plays his mistress without getting thwacked in the chops in the process. Indeed he shows unexpected decency in asking her to be his wife at the end after she's done the dirty on him by running off with a younger man. The end product looks good and sounds good, despite the fundamentally spineless plot and Robert Wise's clichéd direction.

'The result was alright, I guess,' Jim summed it up. He would hardly have said that about *These Wilder Years*, a soap opera of no substantial dimensions whose sole benefit was the presence of the gutsy Barbara Stanwyck opposite Cagney. His steely-eyed steel tycoon, who has mellowed in middle age just sufficiently to look for his long lost illegitimate son, is well-matched stylistically by her fiery adoption home administrator. Where he is ruthlessly icy, she is ethical and determined, preferring to go to court rather than find the boy for his previously unloving father. Eventually the initial friction gives way to romantic involvement, the couple dance the Charleston together and the picture degenerates into hackneyed slush.

Not so Jim's 'comeback', as *Man Of A Thousand Faces* was dubbed by its producers, Universal International. It is another of the biopics which Cagney, with his gift for mimicry, had a special talent for, this time of the silent cinema star, Lon Chaney, the man who virtually invented the horror movie before dying prematurely of cancer in 1930.

Jim was touched by the biography of the son of deaf mutes who grew up to become a vaudevillian (like himself), and a master of cinematic disguises, only to be abandoned by his wife and left to bring up his son, Lon Chaney Junior, on his

Resuming as George M. Cohan opposite Bob Hope's Eddie Foy in *The Seven Little Foys* **(1955), and in rehearsal.**

own. Predictably Jim's preparations were exhaustive and included learning deaf and dumb sign language which he uses effectively several times, notably for prayer, which Lon had said that way from earliest childhood and on his death bed when the disease has destroyed his vocal chords to the point he can no longer speak.

In another sense, the picture is a triumph for the make-up man who worked for as long as three hours before each day's shooting to re-create the special effects Chaney had devised for his many and varied roles. The Hunchback Of Notre Dame disguise, for example, weighed seventy-two pounds and was as impressive in its time as John Hurt's transformation into the Elephant Man is today.

Man of a Thousand Faces has a certain feeling of déjà vu. As in *Yankee Doodle Dandy*, Jeanne Cagney plays the sister to her brother's hero and the warmth between them is clear for all to see. Jim is magnificent in some of his impersonations: as old Lady Murgatroyd, in wig and spectacles, sewing 'her' fingers together to amuse 'her' son; as the Miracle Man, knotted and crippled at one moment, cured by a faith healer the next; and as the hairy hunchback himself. Unfortunately it's not enough and a film that could have been an artistic tour de force is left threadbare by an undistinguished supporting cast, a dismal script and Joseph Pevney's run-of-the-mill direction.

Although, under normal circumstances, Cagney, who felt persecuted by most directors and admired but three or four, wouldn't have had much sympathy for Mr Pevney's inadequacies, he might well have felt they had a bond in common after his next assigment, *Short Cut To Hell*. It was a low budget re-make of *This Gun For Hire*, adapted from Graham Greene's novel, a trite, boringly acted and direly directed work of no importance. Its significance lies only in the fact that James Cagney sat in the canvas chair. He was on screen briefly as himself in a short introductory prologue but controlled proceedings off screen throughout. Many have mused over this unexpected switch to an activity for which he had no possible qualifications and, as the result comprehensively proved, absolutely no flair. Characteristically, it seems, he did it as a favour to a pal, A. C. Lyles, a young and charming B-picture producer who needed a lift into the big time, a shot in the arm that Cagney felt his direction might provide. In the event, it didn't but the good intention was there.

Reflecting on the experience in his autobiography, he wrote, 'Directors, like human beings, come in all sorts: very talented, talented, quasi talented, untalented. It is a profession I have never envied. So when my old friend came to me and asked if I would direct his *Short Cut To Hell*, I was moved to do so out of friendship only. I said

I'd do it if he wanted me to, and he asked me how much I'd charge. 'How about nothing? Is that too much?', I asked him. We shot it in just twenty days, and that was long enough for me. Directing I find a bore; I have no interest in telling other people their business and that is the heart of the job. Some directors tell you your business quite competently; other are unbelievably inept.'

Among them James Francis Cagney Junior, though he didn't admit it. However he soon put the unwelcome experience behind him with his fifth and last Hollywood hoofing picture, *Never Steal Anything Small*. The pity of it is that it is also his worst, a flimsy vehicle with undistinguished songs sprouting out at inopportune moments to interrupt a semi-serious drama about labour problems among stevedores. Cagney plays a gangster stevedore who steals from his employers and rigs elections to make himself a labour leader, a public enemy of a new and chilling kind in Cagney's now ultra-conservative book. The film's strong anti-union attitudes would have shocked erstwhile supporters who still believed Jim's heart to be in the right liberal place but by this time, no one expected anything different.

A consistent feature of Cagney's career was how American-based it was but 1959 saw him make one of his rare working excursions onto foreign soil for *Shake Hands With The Devil*. Originally this reconstruction of the Irish 'Troubles' of 1921, the ones that led to Independence for Eire the following year, was to have been made by a company largely owned by Marlon Brando. Fortunately, given Jim's unconcealed antipathy towards the Method actor he'd never met, the deal fell through. Instead it was whizz kid Michael Anderson who piloted Cagney on this voyage of discovery of the Irish roots he'd never known. He portrays a surgeon turned freedom fighter who becomes totally obsessed with the struggle for independence. The character of Sean Lenihan links violence with mania, a theme Jim had been developing in the decade since *White Heat*. He changes from a civilised doctor into a rabid and blood-thirsty terrorist during the course of some melodramatic adventures involving coffins full of guns and the kidnapping of minor British royals.

Cagney took lessons in Irish brogue from Mr Anderson's secretary but they weren't a hundred percent successful and elements of Americanese creep in at awkward moments. Nor is the film an outright winner despite its star's hardnosed portrait of a pitiless revolutionary, and excellent back-up from Michael Redgrave, Cyril Cusack, Dame Sybil Thorndike and Dana Wynter.

Now he was on the other side of the Atlantic

A musical interlude during Tribute to a Bad Man **opposite Irene Papas (1956).**

104

1844-40

106

— he and Billie had arrived by ship after a stormy November crossing — Jim was strong-armed into visiting London to support a major retrospective of his work at the National Film Theatre. He gave a lecture and supplied cryptic answers to the questions that followed it, replying for example to the familiar one about how often he watched his films with the customary economical comment, 'Once you've finished a job, you've done with it'.

His wife, nicknamed 'the Dorothy Parker of Coldwater Canyon', was more forthcoming. 'He's just a real softie,' she said, in response to a query as to how Jim behaved at home. 'I try not to order him about. He's a sentimental Irishman.' And on their marriage, 'You know, we've stayed married for so long that I think I'm going to charge folks a dollar a time to come and look at us.'

Doing favours for friends was a deeply en-grained Cagney trait, and one who could always persuade him to see things his way was Bob Montgomery. He'd even extracted a promise from Jim that if he ever worked in the hated medium of television, it would be for him. And he collected in 1956, when Jim appeared in *Soldiers From The Wars Returning*, as an Army Sergeant escorting a corpse back from Korea under the banner, Robert Montgomery Presents. Their second association, *The Gallant Hours,* was equally Services-oriented, a re-living of five weeks of the War in the Pacific, and more specifically the battle of Guadalcanal in 1942. The film is a tribute to Fleet Admiral William F. Halsey, the Commander of the U.S. Third Pacific Fleet at the time, and the action is seen through his eyes.

'This film is a labour of love and gratitude to a man who, when the chips were down, performed for us,' said Cagney. 'Bull' Halsey was grateful for the treatment when he saw the completed film just before his death at the age of seventy-five. There is no doubt that Jim's portrait is of an honourable man, compassionate and with a sense of humour, although given to outbursts of emotion and temper. The Cagney Halsey is brooding and introspective, weighed down by the inevitability of sending sailors to their death. Although semi-documentary in style, *The Gallant Hours* is far from being an all-action conventional war movie. The 911 aircraft and seventy-one ships destroyed by the Enterprise while it was under the Fleet Admiral's command are not called on to lend thrills to the dull scenario. Instead Cagney paces the deck, contemplates the ocean and agonises over his crushing responsibilities. Hardly cinematic but it certainly presents Halsey's point of view with telling accuracy.

Jim had certain problems impersonating the

Unmistakeably himself in Man of a Thousand Faces **with Robert Evans (1957).**

'Bull'. Some of his best known sayings, like 'The only good Jap is a dead one' were less than acceptable seventeen years on. Halsey had no striking mannerisms which meant Jim had nothing much to latch onto. At the same time, he had to suppress his more obvious Cagneyisms if the portrayal was to stick so he asked Montgomery to point them out whenever they became intrusive. Nor was Jim helped by his own increasing girth and diminishing looks, elements which had to be concealed by such cunning devices as having him cover his swimsuit with a full-length beach robe while back to camera before turning round to continue the action.

Other faces in a thousand.

The narration which seeks to explain a self-evident plot as the events unfold in flashback from the starting point of Halsey's final leave-taking of his crew, is a fundamental weakness in what is anyway an exasperatingly slow film. So too is the intrusive hymnal music but Cagney's 'Bull' makes it. 'There is no braggadocio in it, not straining for bold or sharp effects,' wrote Bosley Crowther in more fanciful vein than usual. 'It is one of the quietest, most reflective, subtlest jobs that Mr Cagney has ever done.'

The sensitive sounding board of Hollywood gossip had been reverberating for several years with rumours of Cagney's retirement but never so resonantly as after *The Gallant Hours*. However he was persuaded into the arena for yet another 'comeback' by a telephone call from Billy Wilder. The project was *One, Two, Three*, a Cold War comedy set in West Berlin, a breakneck series of shouting matches, chases and verbal contortions. The jokes, whether sexual or political, are prejudiced and dated and it is only the fact that the film is the fastest either of these mercurial talents ever made that makes it memorable.

Jim plays a Coca Cola executive hell bent on clawing his way up the ladder, an ascent that may be interrupted if he fails to stop a spoiled Southern teenager (Pamela Tiffin) from marrying an East Berlin Marxist (Horst Buchholz). It is fitting that this, Jim's pre-retirement role, is a veteran's mirror image of Tom Powers, a bombastic corporate fat cat whose raison d'être is self-advancement, no matter what the cost in human terms. The film took some making and the relations between the king of rat-a-tat-tat and one

of the most frenetic directors in the business was not always smooth. Sometimes fifty takes were needed for a single scene while Cagney, faced with complicated monologues delivered to him for memorising the night before they were to be shot, was less word perfect than normal.

Nor did he and Horst Buchholz hit it off, as Jim recalled in his autobiography when he wrote: 'It is very interesting that not until the very end of my career did I meet an unco-operative fellow actor. As I review the pictures I've been in, I realise that each and every actor I worked with had a part in shaping my summary views on acting. We all worked together rewardingly with what I hope was mutual enrichment. I never had the slightest difficulty with a fellow actor until the making of *One, Two, Three*. In that picture, Horst Buchholz tried all kinds of scene-stealing didoes, and I had to depend on Billy Wilder to take some steps to correct this kid. If Billy hadn't, I was going to knock Buchholz on his ass, which at several points I would have been very happy to do.'

It never came to that and the film, one of Wilder's worst, was eventually finished. 'Plenty of speed, but not much pace' was how Penelope Gilliat summed up the consensus opinion. Others were even less complimentary. 'The Saturday Review' critic, for example, wrote, 'Cagney, I fear, has done Wilder an ill service. He shouts his way through the entire movie, bellowing and bowling over all opposition. After a while, I found myself flinching every time he gathered his breath. A man just can't keep that up without strain to the vital organs.'

Despite those persistent Hollywood rumours,

Above and right, Pepsi Cola magnate extraordinaire in Billy Wilder's *One, Two, Three* **(1961).**

Cagney himself has always maintained that he didn't know *One, Two, Three* would be his swan song until he was mid-way through it. The revelation came to him one sunny afternoon in Munich (where it was being made) when he received a letter from a pal, Rolie Winters, to whom he'd lent his boat. Enclosed was a photo of Rolie and his friends sitting on the deck and raising their glasses to their benefactor. 'Nice you are gainfully employed,' read the caption.

'And didn't they look smug,' Jim recalled. 'I savoured their enjoyment. At least for this one moment I was sharing some of their pleasure; I

was out in the sun and the green was green as green and the air was clean. I was experiencing this part of my day with pleasure. Then the assistant director came and said, 'Mr. Cagney, we're ready'. So inside the studio I went and as they closed the giant doors behind me and I found myself in that great black cavern with just a few spotlights dotted here and there, I said to myself, 'Well, this is it. This is the end. I'm finished.' I knew at that moment that I would never bother about acting any more. After *One, Two, Three* was completed, I didn't even bother to see it. And for the simplest of reasons: I'm just not that much interested. I had the career — it was fine, I enjoyed it, but it was over.'

Or so he thought for twenty years . . .

CHAPTER 7
FARMER JIM

When Bop Hope asked Jeanne Cagney how Jim could retire after three decades in pictures, she replied that it was what he'd been preparing for for thirty years. And she was right. In the mid Fifties, he'd bought a second farm, in Dutchess County, New York State, partly as a refuge from the fashionable hordes who had closed in on Martha's Vineyard, destroying the tranquillity he'd appreciated for twenty years, and partly because the new property had a six acre lake.

There in the summers after his retirement, Cagney fulfilled a dream of building his own house — admittedly with the considerable assistance of Gerald W. Papendick, a versatile contractor from California who was initially imported for moral support. How it worked was that Jim, having designed a simple house and the materials to construct it out of, would pick a stone and start to put it in place. Then 'Pappy', as he was nicknamed, would tell him it was the wrong one and select another which invariably fitted much better. The end result was idiosyncratic and astonished the neighbours with its lack of pretension, especially in an area where there were lots of fancy properties.

But Cagney had his reason: 'The plain truth,' he said, 'is that I don't like plush houses, I don't like fancy houses. I like to be able to sit down and put my feet up whenever I feel like it. Big handsome places to me are a burden.'

This farm was the centre of Jim's cattle and horse breeding programmes and he also grew the corn and hay to feed them. It is perhaps fortunate that acting was thrust upon him for the farms were never commercially viable though he scoured specialist magazines for new ideas and travelled even as far as distant South Dakota to buy Western Scottish Highland cattle, a beef breed whose long red hair made Jim feel that destiny had linked them through pigmentation. Only later, when it was pointed out by a well-wisher in the meat trade that once the hide comes off, one slab of beef is very much like another, and not about to raise a higher price because of its lost beauty on the hoof, did he realise that the expedition was more of an indulgence than an investment. So most of the

A man and his horse.

112

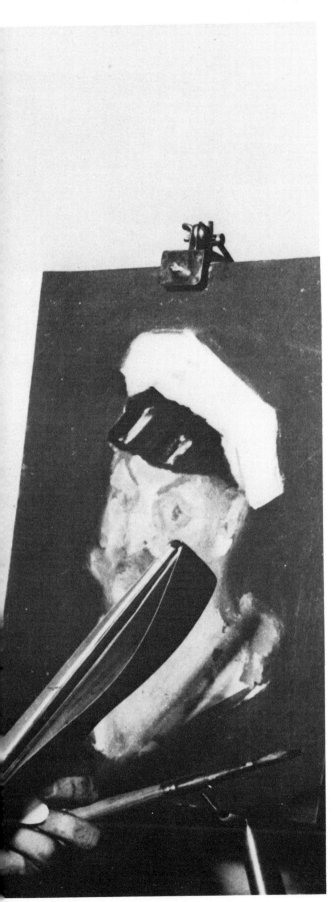

Highlands went to the market, leaving the few survivors to decorate Jim's lakescape.

The horses were a more serious matter. Not only had they been his favourite animals since those far off days when he'd ridden New York's horse-powered streetcars but he'd been breeding them for years even before his retirement. The Morgan, a tough functional horse that can be worked or ridden, was his favourite among the favourites and it was these he specialised in. At one stage, he attempted to fine down their large but honest heads by using an Arab stallion but that didn't work too well. Nor did an excursion into trotters and pacers. However he rode and drove himself, and was a regular spectator at horse shows and race meetings.

In the summer, Jim and Billie divided their time between Dutchess County and Martha's Vineyard so that he could indulge in his other sporting passion — sailing. For years, he'd kept his 1907 eighty-six foot standard-type schooner, the Martha, on the West Coast, but eastern waters required a shallow draft craft. Accordingly Cagney commissioned a forty-three foot Chesapeke Bay Bugeye, a ketch rig boat which drew just 3′ 9″ and so was ideal for exploring the rocky inlets around the island. In fact he was no long-distance mariner by inclination, not least because he was prone to seasickness, and preferred pottering around within sight of land on the East Coast to the more open sailing he'd become accumstomed to in California.

His other hobbies were writing poetry which came more from the heart than the head and painting at which he was rather better. He'd kept up his youthful enthusiasm for drawing and over the years he'd often amused his friends with perceptive cartoons but it wasn't until the late Fifties that he took himself an art master. He owed a lot to his friend, the television presenter Jack Bailey, for an introduction to Sergei Bongart, a long-term Russian immigrant who he described as 'a great painter, a great human being'. Initially the teacher thought his pupil was 'just another actor dilettante' but he was proved wrong on lesson one, the drawing of a still life in black and white, which Jim took two solid months to perfect.

From then on, he took regular lessons and attended Bongart's summer school in Idaho. The two men had a remarkably similar perception of art which made their meetings highly enjoyable, so much so that they often had trouble getting down to work. On occasion they went further afield, to Europe for example, where they shared their delight in painting and living like bums in

The artist at work.

less salubrious — but perhaps more colourful — surroundings than America could offer. Over the years, Jim's paintings improved considerably but he was never tempted to sell them — that would have been unfair to struggling artists who couldn't conjure up a famous name as a marketing device. His only recorded sale was to Johnny Carson who paid 5,500 dollars for a still life, painted on a piece of shirt cardboard but the proceeds went to SHARE, a charity for gifted children.

Jim may have looked on himself as an Easterner and a farmer first and second, but those thirty years of escape from the hell of New York winters had left its mark and he was never loathe to return to California when the weather closed in. To that end he kept his house in Coldwater Canyon and bought another one in the desert outside Palm Springs. As ever, he was reluctant to travel by air and his transcontinental trips in cars he invariably drove at a measured pace gave him opportunities to learn to love the landscape in each state as it unfolded before him. They also gave him cause to hate what he calls 'the senseless destruction of the land.'

Everywhere he went, he saw man-made blight caused by the hated bulldozer, and that included the highways he drove along. Often he felt that the number of lanes was quite unjustifiable, especially when they'd been added later for no discernible reason. As an ardent conservationist ever since that long-lost holiday in his aunt's house in Flatbush, he never ceased to be horrified by the changes that a burgeoning population had imposed on his beloved countryside in the intervening years. In particular he abhorred the building of huge roads and extravagant interchanges, a process he saw as legitimised highway robbery, a despicable racket designed to keep the road builders in profitable business forever at the taxpayer's expense.

He, of course, has done his bit to peddle the great illusory American dream over thirty years of prime screen exposure and so contributed to the condition of his country with its endless straggling neon-lit suburbia and its insatiable lust for making easy bucks. However he, unlike most of his peers, has always been prepared to turn out for the cause. On occasion he came out of retirement to speak on the subject, narrating several radio programmes on soil conservation, giving a lecture at the University of Maine and lending his voice to the General Electric Theatre for its 'Ballad of Smokey the Bear', an animated fantasy which it co-produced with the U.S. Department of Agriculture.

Less admirably, political commitment could also tempt him out of obscurity and in 1962 he narrated a crude documentary, a government propaganda film produced by C.B.S. for the Defense Department and called Road to the Wall.

It outlined Communist takeovers and purges with the grim purpose of warning Americans to keep their eyes open for danger signals on the home front, a deliberate invitation to witch hunting which Jim should have been ashamed to be associated with. In 1968 his old mate, A. C. Lyles, the man who had inveigled him into directing Short Cut To Hell, was again successful in persuading him to speak the introduction to another abortive project, Arizona Bushwackers, an indifferent Western starring Howard Keel, for which he was fortunate to receive an unobtrusive credit.

The fact that Cagney did these voiceovers but refused to appear in front of the cameras gave rise to speculation that he had become grossly fat. Pat O'Brien refered to him as 'Mr. Five-By-Five' in his autobiography and the abstemious Jim himself admitted to an unwise passion for root beer (an American soft drink) that tended to put on the lard. However his general health remained excellent which he ascribes to continual use of the 'old dancing board'. When his brother Harry died in 1964, he took himself off for a check up and received the encouraging news that he was in exceptionally good nick for a sixty-five-year-old. Could they, the doctors asked, use him as a guinea pig in certain tests designed to establish why he'd lasted so well? They never revealed the answer but he gives credit to non-stop activity.

He ascribed his well being to his ability to preserve his sense of wonder and maintain an interest in everything that went on around him. He was also careful to instil those values in his children, Jim and Casey. He exhorted them never to take anything for granted nor to assume that anything in life was commonplace. The alternative to a sense of wonder by his book was disinterest, boredom and death. Whether his children learnt his lessons well or not, he certainly profited from them himself.

Fat or not, Jim certainly turned down some plum offers. The sternest temptation was Alfred Doolittle, the dancing dustman immortalised by Stanley Holloway in George Cukor's My Fair Lady in 1964. Not only could he have written his own pay cheque but it was a prime hoofing part and Cukor, having got his phone number off Katherine Hepburn, pursued him relentlessly. 'He wouldn't take no for an answer,' Jim recalled. 'I gently tried to discourage him, but he wouldn't stay discouraged. Eventually they went on without me, and that was fine because Stanley Holloway is a wonderful entertainer and he was great. That, then, is the only time I've had a slight tug to go back.'

The next year Samual Bronston approached him for the abortive The French Revolution and his old friend, Jack Lemmon, tried to enlist him for Kotch in 1972. Then came Francis Ford

Coppola, riding high after *The Godfather,* and with plans for part two; they included James Cagney and the whizz kid director arrived in person in a private jet to plead his cause. The two professionals met over breakfast, cooked by Jim at seven o'clock in the morning in the Dutchess County farmhouse, drove behind a matched pair of his horses through the autumn woods and inspected his Morgan stud. They discussed the movie business but *Godfather II* was not mentioned until Coppola was on the point of leaving. 'Mr. Cagney,' he said in farewell, 'I came here hoping to talk you out of retirement to come and do this thing with us. But what I'm going to tell you is that I haven't talked you out of retirement, you've talked me into it!'

So life went on its peaceful satisfying way. His brother Ed had died suddenly in 1968 but the new generation was growing up to give continuity to the family life Cagney loved so much. It was probably not his bit part in *The Gallant Hours* that inspired his son to join the Marines, but that was the career he chose and in due course Marine Corporal James Cagney married Marine Corporal Jill Inness. Casey Cagney too was married, to Jack Thomas, and both couples produced grandchildren for the delighted Jim.

In 1974 the routine was shattered briefly when Cagney was asked if he'd accept the second ever American Film Institute Life Achievement Award. Once again the intermediary was A. C. Lyles and once again he was able to bend the stubborn Irishman to his will. The award, which had gone to John Ford the year before, was given to 'an individual whose talents have in a fundamental way contributed to the film making arts, whose accomplishments have been acknowledged by scholars, critics, professional peers and the general public and whose body of work has stood the test of time.'

Fair enough. James Cagney was clearly eligible and he decided to accept it as a thank you to the industry that had put the groceries on the table in such abundance. He'd always been vocally scornful of awards but he realised that the American Film Institute wasn't acting altruistically when they offered him this one. They needed a peg to hang their annual fund-raising event on, and he was it. As the money was essential if they were to keep up their good work, he was prepared to come out of hiding and get it for them. Once having agreed, Jim addressed the task with his customary thoroughness. He moved back to Coldwater Canyon and swam and tanned himself into shape for the show. He also admitted a trickle of reporters and photographers, dutifully selling the AFI message to every interviewer.

The banquet itself took place in the Century Plaza Hotel on March 13th in front of television cameras which transmitted it to fifty million viewers. It was a glittering Hollywood occasion as the old guard and the new breed of pop and television personalities thronged together in tribute to the 'feisty little Irishman' as Master of Ceremonies, Frank Sinatra, introduced the guest of honour. Among them were friends from the Irish 'Mafia', Ralph Bellamy, Frank McHugh and Allen Jenkins, as well as 'grapefruit girl', Mae Clarke.

The accolades came thick and fast: from Bob Hope who told how Jim had taught him to dance; from George C. Scott, who'd refused to cross America to pick up his Oscar for Patton but had no hesitation in turning out for Jim; from Doris Day, who recalled the happy days on *Love Me Or Leave Me;* from Jack Lemmon, Shirley Maclaine and John Wayne; and from Ronald Reagan, then Governor of California, who suggested people should forget his own films and honour Jim's. Sound advice indeed!

Frank Gorshin, Cagney's best imitator, did his trouser-hitching routine, the one Jim had borrowed from a man he used to see on the corner of Seventy-eighth Street and First Avenue when he was twelve years old, and later made into film history as Rocky Sullivan in *Angels with Dirty Faces.* Frank Sinatra did his bit too by adding special lyrics to his hit, My Way: 'James Cagney is the perfect whizz,' he crooned. 'He did it his way.' The applause was deafening.

Then it was Jim's turn. White-haired and rather more portly than before, he nevertheless gave the lie to those accusations of grossness. His voice shook with emotion on his first public appearance in thirteen years and the tears that had flowed so easily throughout his life were never far away. Nevertheless he was able to deliver a short agile dance, a long speech of thanks to many people he felt indebted to in the business and another firm denial of that 'Dirty Rat', followed by a Cary Grant impersonation that brought the house down.

Even on this day of celebration, he gave proof of the waste not, want not philosophy instilled by the indomitable Carrie in all her sons, by writing his speech on shirt cards, just as he had painted Johnny Carson's picture. As the organisers didn't want his image spoiled by glasses and as he couldn't see without them, there were a great number of cards, economically covered on both sides with the names he needed printed in block capitals. To his great regret, he mislaid one whole side so a number of benefactors go unthanked to this day, but that was his only slip-up on an occasion which raised 45,000 dollars for the AFI's educational and historical programme.

By Jim's book that made coming out of the closet very worthwhile — and he returned to his self-imposed obscurity well satisfied with his night's work.

CHAPTER 8
BACK IN HARNESS

When James Cagney was a youngster on the Warner's lot, he'd been asked to fill out a studio questionnaire which included, among many other items, the heading 'ambition'. Under it, Jim had written, 'To retire to the backwoods permanently.' Thirty years later he'd done just that and Hollywood expected to see no more of him. Those who had tried to tempt him back had had a hundred percent failure rate — until the Czech Milos Forman came on the scene, casting around for his New York Police Commissioner Rheinlander Waldo in *Ragtime*. And, to the amazement of the film world, answer came there, yes.

How come, Cagney was asked, Forman succeeded where Cukor, Coppola and others had been shown the door? 'Doctor's orders,' he replied. 'Mine said, "Get this man working." I have to keep my batteries charged to keep going.' The ravages of time had been fairly kind to the spry eighty-one-year-old but a mild stroke he suffered in the mid-Seventies combined with diabetes which went undiagnosed over ten years had stiffened his body and impaired his mobility. However his speech was as crisp as ever and it isn't hard to detect a sly delight in his astonishing acceptance of Forman's bait.

'I had everything a man could want,' he told a reporter, 'and then one day, completely by chance, I met my good friend and neighbour Milos Forman and we chatted as we walked along the path between our properties. He told me he'd soon be starting shooting on *Ragtime* and jokingly asked me if I wouldn't like to take part. I replied in the same vein and we separated. Nothing changed over the next few weeks but I found I was becoming more and more intrigued by the project. Finally curiosity won. I went to see my neighbour and told him, "Okay, let's go with this film".'

Ragtime, based on E. L. Doctorow's best seller about changing attitudes in New York around the turn of the century, took Jim straight back to his Lower East Side roots. It is an ensemble piece that examimes the phenomena of the day with perspicacity and style. A man who makes ingenious paper cut-outs in a street market of the kind Jim would have roamed as a boy becomes an

Back in harness after 20 years' 'retirement', as Police Commissioner Rheinlander Waldo in *Ragtime* **(1981).**

The killing goes on. *Ragtime* (1981).

RT-11794

Ragtime: **Milos Forman directs.**

overnight sensation as a film director; an unknown girl, likewise, becomes a star; members of a middle class family, representing the emerging bourgeoisie, grapple in their different ways with new elements in their society, among them a black girl who leaves her baby under their blackberry bush; and the baby's father, a bright young black with a brand new motor car, gets a going over from prejudiced Irish firemen intent on protecting their entrenched position from the likes of him.

In those days, urban terrorism wasn't the common occurrence it is today, and it is intro-

duced and developed here as the climax of a fascinating film. With it comes Rheinlander Waldo, the Police Commissioner in charge of stamping it out. Cagney is a bulldog in the part, jowly and slow moving but fast talking, a bastion of brutal law and order in a changing world. He appears briefly at the introductory banquet at which Stanford White (Norman Mailer) is shot, then holds the centre screen through the last third of the long film. It is a typical late Cagney role, a

hard liner whose determination to maintain the status quo causes him to break his word and perpetrate the final dishonourable execution.

The schedule required two months' work in England in the autumn of 1980 and the rumours from the rigidly closed set were that Jim, though often in pain, was doing fine. 'It's a long part for a man of my age,' he said at the time, 'but whenever anyone has proposed a tough role, I've always said, "I'll do it" . . . and I always have. My

A rare television appearance on the BBC TV Parkinson Show in February 1982.

doctor thought a bit of work wouldn't do me any harm, and in fact since shooting started, I've lost several pounds and I feel considerably fitter.'

Forman's excitement at his coup and his admiration for his star were unbounded. 'I would have let him play Evelyn Nesbitt if he'd wanted to,' he exclaimed. 'His instincts are phenomenal.

As a director, I don't have to tell him a thing. I know the word is abused but I really think James is some kind of genius.'

'Is that a joke?' Cagney demanded, when this high praise was relayed to him. 'Acting is a job for me, just as it has always been. The thing to do is to try to give the audience something to take away with them.' So it was business as usual but the presence of Pat O'Brien in a minor role in the *Ragtime* line-up made it something of a joyful old timer's reunion. The pair stole the show at the Queen Mother's Eightieth Birthday Royal Command Performance in London in November 1980 and she broke protocol afterwards by going backstage to greet her transatlantic contemporaries and congratulate them on their performances.

Jim made several appearances in November, 1981 when the picture opened in New York, among them one on the Today Show, presented by Gene Shalit, on which he finally laid a ghost by saying 'you dirty rat' for the first time in public. He returned to London in February for the British premiere, doing a guest spot on the Parkinson show alongside Pat O'Brien and proving his verbal pace with a slick recall of Ricky Sullivan's dilemma. Was he or was he not yellow when he went to the chair? As usual Jim didn't give the answer. Forty years on, we must still decide for ourselves.

Recently he celebrated his eighty-third birthday and his diamond wedding. 'Billie,' he said in tribute, 'is a truly remarkable wife. When we were married, I impressed on her that she would never have to come to my assistance — and she's been doing so ever since!'

Now the Cagneys are back on the farm, the centre of a warm and admiring circle of family and friends. Survivors of the old guard are regular visitors as is John Travolta, representing the new generation. The suspicion is that Jim's retirement will never be so total again. There are rumours of a biopic, with Mikhail Baryshnikov poised on his points to do for James Cagney what he himself did for George M. Cohan in *Yankee Doodle Dandy*. There is a certain irony in a superstar of the Russian ballet, trained with everything the system had to offer, playing the self-taught hoofer who began his dancing career in skirts, which makes it the kind of ultimate accolade that might suit Jim very well. Nor is it certain that the cameras will never turn on him again. Another Czech ex-patriot director, Ivan Passer, is making *The Eagle of Broadway* and the part of Bat Masterson, the legendary Indian hunter, professional gambler and scout who stood at the side of Wyatt Earp before becoming a sports reporter in later life, is Jim's for the asking.

Does life begin — again— at eighty? For James Cagney, the answer must be yes.

Sinner's Holiday
(1930) Warner Bros. 60 minutes
Director John G. Adolfi
Screenplay Harvey Thew and
George Rosenor (from Marie
Baumer's play, Penny Arcade)
Cast James Cagney (as Harry
Delano) with Grant Withers,
Evalyn Knapp, Joan Blondell,
Lucille La Verne and Noel
Madison
Doorway to Hell
(G.B. A Handful of Clouds)
(1930) Warner Bros. 77 minutes
Director Archie Mayo *Screenplay*
George Rosenor *Cast* James
Cagney (as Steve Mileaway) with
Lew Ayres, Charles Judels,
Dorothy Matthews, Leon
Janney, Robert Elliott and
Kenneth Thomson
Other Men's Woman
(1931) Warner Bros. 70 minutes
Director William A. Wellman
Screenplay Maude Fulton and
William K. Wells. *Cast* James
Cagney (as Ed) with Grant
Withers, Mary Astor, Regis
Toomey, Joan Blondell and Fred
Kohler
The Millionaire
(1931) Warner Bros, 82 minutes
Director John G. Adolfi
Screenplay Julian Josephson and
Maude T. Powell *Cast* James
Cagney (Schofield, an insurance
salesman) with George Arliss,
Evalyn Knapp, David Manner,
Bramwell Fletcher, Florence
Arliss and Noah Beery
The Public Enemy
(G.B. Enemies of the Public)
(1931) Warner Bros. 74 minutes
Director William A. Wellman
Screenplay Kubec Glasmon, John
Bright and Harvey Thew (from a
Glasmon and Bright story) *Cast*

James Cagney (as Tom Powers)
with Jean Harlow, Mae Clarke,
Joan Blondell, Edward Woods,
Beryl Mercer, Donald Cook and
Mia Marvin
Smart Money
(1931) Warner Bros. 90 minutes
Director Alfred E. Green
Screenplay Kubec Glasmon, John
Bright, Lucien Hubbard and
Joseph Jackson (from a Hubbard
and Jackson story) *Cast* James
Cagney (as Jack, the barber's
assistant) with Edward G.
Robinson, Noel Francis, Morgan
Wallace, Evalyn Knapp, Paul
Porcasi, Maurice Black,
Margaret Livingston, Clark
Burroughs and Boris Karloff
Blonde Crazy
(G.B. Larceny Lane)
(1931) Warner Bros. 73 minutes
Director Roy del Ruth *Screenplay*
Kubec Glasmon and John Bright
(from their own story) *Cast*
James Cagney (as Bert Harris)
with Joan Blondell, Louis
Calhern, Noel Francis, Guy
Kibbee and Raymond Milland
Taxi
(1932) Warner Bros. 70 minutes
Director Roy del Ruth *Screenplay*
Kubec Glasmon and John Bright
(from Kenyon Nicholson's play,
The Blind Spot) *Cast* James
Cagney (as Matt Nolan) with
Loretta Young, George E.
Stone, Guy Kibbee, Ray Cooke,
David Landau, Leila Bennet,
Matt McHugh and George Raft
The Crowd Roars
(1932) Warner Bros. 85 minutes
Director Howard Hawks
Screenplay Kubec Glasmon and
John Bright with Niven Busch
(from a Hawks story) *Cast* James
Cagney (as Joe Greer, racing

motorist) with Joan Blondell,
Ann Dvorak, Eric Linden, Guy
Kibbee, Frank McHugh, William
Arnold, Regis Toomey and Leo
Nomis
Winner Take All
(1932) Warner Bros. 68 minutes
Director Roy Del Ruth
Screenplay Wilson Mizner and
Robert Lord (from a magazine
story by Gerald Beaumont) *Cast*
James Cagney (as Jim Kane, a
boxer) with Marian Nixon,
Virginia Bruce, Guy Kibbee,
Clarence Muse, Dickie Moore,
Allan Lane and John Roche
Hard to Handle
(1933) Warner Bros. 75 minutes
Director Mervyn LeRoy
Screenplay Wilson Mizner and
Robert Lord *Cast* James Cagney
(as Lefty Merill, con artist) with
Mary Brian, Ruth Donnelly,
Allen Jenkins, Claire Dodd,
Gavin Gordon, Emma Dunn and
Matt McHugh
Picture Snatcher
(1933) Warner Bros. 76 minutes
Director Lloyd Bacon *Screenplay*
Allen Rivkin and P. J. Wolfson
Cast James Cagney (as Danny
Kean, photographer) with Ralph
Bellamy, Patricia Ellis, Alice
White, Ralf Harolde, Robert
Emmett O'Connor, Robert
Barrat and George Pat Collins
The Mayor of Hell
(1933) Warner Bros. 85 minutes
Director Archie Mayo *Screenplay*
Edward Chodorov *Cast* James
Cagney (as Patsy Gargan, a well-
intentioned hoodlum) with
Madge Evans, Allen Jenkins,
Dudley Digges, Frankie Darro,
Farina and Dorothy Peterson
Footlight Parade
(1933) Warner Bros. 100 minutes
Director Lloyd Bacon and Busby
Berkeley *Screenplay* Manuel Seff
and James Seymour *Cast* James
Cagney (as Chester Kent, a
hoofing impresario) with Joan
Blondell, Ruby Keeler, Dick

Powell, Guy Kibbee, Ruth
Donnelly, Claire Dodd, Hugh
Herbert, Frank McHugh and
Arthur Hohl
Lady Killer
(1933) Warner Bros. 76 minutes
Director Roy del Ruth *Screenplay*
Ben Markson and Lillie Hayward
Cast James Cagney (as Dan
Quigley, a con-man turned film
star) with Mae Clarke, Leslie
Fenton, Margaret Lindsay,
Henry O'Neill, Willard
Robertson and Bud Flanagan
Jimmy the Gent
(1934) Warner Bros. 70 minutes
Director Michael Curtiz
Screenplay Bertram Milhauser
Cast James Cagney (as Jimmy
Corrigan, systematic fortune
hunter) with Bette Davis, Alice
White, Allen Jenkins, Arthur
Hohl, Alan Dienhart and Philip
Reed
He was her Man
(1934) Warner Bros. 70 minutes
Director Lloyd Bacon *Screenplay*
Tom Buckingham and Niven
Busch *Cast* James Cagney (as
Flicker Hayes, a gangster-on-the-
run) with Joan Blondell, Victor
Jory, Frank Craven, Harold
Huber and Russell Hopton.
Here Comes the Navy
(1934) Warner Bros. 86 minutes
Director Lloyd Bacon *Screenplay*
Ben Markson and Earl Baldwin
Cast James Cagney (as Chesty
O'Connor, a seaman hero) with
Pat O'Brien, Gloria Stuart,
Frank McHugh, Dorothy Tree,
Robert Barrat and Willard
Layson
The St. Louis Kid
(G.B. A Perfect Weekend)
(1934) Warner Bros. 67 minutes
Director Ray Enright *Screenplay*
Warren Duff and Seton I. Miller
Cast James Cagney (as Eddie
Kennedy, long-distance truck
driver) with Patricia Ellis, Allen
Jenkins, Robert Barrat, Hobart
Cavanaugh, Spencer Charters

Director Anatole Litvak instructs Cagney and Ann Sheridan in *City for Conquest* (1941).

and Addison Richards

Devil Dogs of Air
(1935) Warner Bros. 86 minutes *Director* Lloyd Bacon *Screenplay* Malcolm Stuart Boylan and Earl Baldwin *Cast* James Cagney (as Tommy O'Toole, a reckless stunt flyer) with Pat O'Brien, Frank McHugh, Margaret Lindsay, Helen Lowell, John Arledge, Robert Barrat and Russell Hicks

G-Men
(1935) Warner Bros. 85 minutes *Director* William Keighley *Screenplay* Seton I. Miller, from Gregory Rogers' book, Public Enemy No. 1 *Cast* James Cagney (as James 'Brick' Davis, lawyer turned FBI agent) with Ann Dvorak, Margaret Lindsay, Robert Armstrong, Barton MacLane, Lloyd Nolan, William Harrigan and Russell Hopton

The Irish in Us
(1935) Warner Bros. 84 minutes *Director* Lloyd Bacon *Screenplay* Earl Baldwin *Cast* James Cagney (as Danny O'Hara, errant boxing manager) with Pat O'Brien, Olivia de Havilland, Frank McHugh, Allen Jenkins, Mary Gordon, J. Farrell MacDonald and Thomas Jackson

A Midsummer Night's Dream
(1935) Warner Bros. 132 minutes *Director* Max Reinhardt and William Dieterle *Screenplay* Charles Kenyon and Mary McCall Junior, from William Shakespeare's play *Cast* James Cagney (as Bottom) with Dick Powell, Joe E. Brown, Mickey Rooney, Olivia de Havilland, Frank McHugh, Hugh Herbert, Ian Hunter, Victor Jory and Ross Alexander

Frisco Kid
(1935) Warner Bros. 77 minutes *Director* Lloyd Bacon *Screenplay* Warren Duff and Seton I. Miller *Cast* James Cagney (as Bat Morgan, a Barbary Coast seaman) with Margaret Lindsay, Ricardo Cortez, Lily Damita, Donald Woods, Barton MacLane, George E. Stone and Addison Richards

Ceiling Zero
(1935) Warner Bros. 95 minutes *Director* Howard Hawks *Screenplay* Frank Wead, from his own play *Cast* James Cagney (as Dizzy Davis, ace aviator) with Pat O'Brien, June Travis, Stuart Erwin, Henry Wadsworth, Isabel Jewell and Barton MacLane

Great Guy
(G.B. Pluck of the Irish)
(1936) Grand National. 75 minutes
Director John G. Blystone *Screenplay* Henry McCarthy, Henry Johnson, James Edward Grant and Harry Ruskin *Cast* James Cagney (as Johnny Cave, campaigner on behalf of the little guy) with Mae Clarke, James Burke, Edward Brophy, Henry Kolker, Bernadene Hayes and Edward J. McNamara

Something to Sing About
(1937) Grand National. 85 minutes
Director Victor Schertzinger *Screenplay* Austin Parker *Cast* James Cagney (as Terry Rooney, a New York bandleader who goes to Hollywood) with Evelyn Daw, William Frawley, Mona Barrie, Gene Lockhart, James Newill, Harry Barris and Candy Candido

Boy Meets Girl
(1938) Warner Bros. 80 minutes *Director* Lloyd Bacon *Screenplay* Bella and Sam Spewack from their own play *Cast* James Cagney (as Robert Law a screenplay writer who makes a baby into a star) with Pat O'Brien, Marie Wilson, Ralph Bellamy, Frank McHugh, Dick Foran, Bruce Lester, Ronald Reagan, Paul Clark and Penny Singleton

Angels with Dirty Faces
(1938) Warner Bros. 97 minutes *Director* Michael Curtiz *Screenplay* John Wexley and Warren Duff *Cast* James Cagney (as Rocky Sullivan, gangster and youth idol) with Pat O'Brien,

Humphrey Bogart, Ann Sheridan, George Bancroft, Billy Halop, Bobby Jordan, Leo Gorcey, Bernard Punsley, Gabriel Dell, Huntz Hall, Frankie Burke, William Tracy, Oscar O'Shea, Edward Pawley, William Pawley, Jim Hamilton, Earl Dwire, Jack Perrin and Mary Gordon

The Oklahoma Kid
(1939) Warner Bros. 85 minutes *Director* Lloyd Bacon *Screenplay* Warren Duff, Robert Buckner and Edward E. Paramore *Cast* James Cagney (as Jim Kincaid, the good cowboy) with Humphrey Bogart, Rosemary Lane, Donald Crisp, Harvey Stephens, Hugh Sothern, Charles Middleton and Ward Bond

Each Dawn I Die
(1939) Warner Bros. 92 minutes *Director* William Keighley *Screenplay* Norman Reilly Raine, Warren Duff and Charles Perry, from Jerome Odlum's novel *Cast* James Cagney (as a newspaper man who is unjustly imprisoned) with George Raft, Jane Bryan, George Bancroft, Maxie Rosenbloom, Stanley Ridges, Alan Baxter, Victor Jory, John Wray, Edward Pawley and Willard Robertson

The Roaring Twenties
(1939) Warner Bros. 104 minutes *Director* Raoul Walsh *Screenplay* Jerry Wald, Richard Macaulay and Robert Rossen *Cast* James Cagney (as Eddie Bartlett, soldier turned liquor baron turned wino) with Humphrey Bogart, Priscilla Lane, Jeffrey Lynn, Frank McHugh, Gladys George, Paul Kelly, Elisabeth Risdon, Ed Keane and Joseph Sawyer

The Fighting 69th
(1940) Warner Bros. 90 minutes *Director* William Keighley *Screenplay* Norman Reilly Raine, Fred Niblo Jr. and Dean Franklin *Cast* James Cagney (as Jerry Plunkett, a cowardly soldier turned hero) with Pat O'Brien,

George Brent, Jeffrey Lynn, Alan Hale, Frank McHugh, Dennis Morgan, Dick Foran, William Lundigan, Guinn Williams, Henry O'Neill, John Litel and Sammy Cohen

Torrid Zone
(1940) Warner Bros. 88 minutes *Director* William Keighley *Screenplay* Richard Macaulay and Jerry Wald *Cast* James Cagney (as Nick Butler, trouble shooter) with Pat O'Brien, Ann Sheridan, Andy Devine, Helen Vinson, Jerome Cowan, George Tobias and George Reeves

City for Conquest
(1941) Warner Bros. 101 minutes *Director* Anatole Litvak *Screenplay* John Wexley, from Aben Kandel's novel *Cast* James Cagney (as Danny Kenny, an amiable trucker who becomes a boxer) with Ann Sheridan, Frank Craven, Donald Crisp, Arthur Kennedy, Frank McHugh, George Tobias, Elia Kazan, Jerome Cowan and Anthony Quinn

The Strawberry Blonde
(1941) Warner Bros. 97 minutes *Director* Raoul Walsh *Screenplay* Julius J. Epstein and Philip G. Epstein, from James Hagan's play, One Sunday Afternoon *Cast* James Cagney (as Biff Grimes, an honest over-emotional dentist who lands up in prison) with Olivia de Havilland, Rita Hayworth, Alan Hale, George Tobias, Jack Carson, Una O'Connor, George Reeves, Lucile Fairbanks, Edward McNamara and Herbert Heywood

The Bride Came C.O.D.
(1941) Warner Bros. 92 minutes *Director* William Keighley *Screenplay* Julius J. Epstein and Philip G. Epstein *Cast* James Cagney (as Steve Collins, an aviator in pursuit of an heiress) with Bette Davis, Stuart Erwin, Jack Carson, George Tobias, Eugene Pallette, Harry Davenport, William Frawley, Edward Brophy and Harry Holman

Captain of the Clouds
(1942) Warner Bros. 113 minutes *Director* Michael Curtiz *Screenplay* Arthur T. Horman, Richard Macaulay and Norman Reilly Raine *Cast* James Cagney (as Brian MacLean, a heroic Canadian pilot in World War II) with Dennis Morgan, Brenda Marshall, Alan Hale, George Tobias, Reginald Gardiner, W. A. Bishop, Reginald Denny, Russell Arms and Paul Cavanagh

Yankee Doodle Dandy
(1942) Warner Bros. 126 minutes *Director* Michael Curtiz *Screenplay* Robert Buckner and Edmund Joseph *Cast* James Cagney (as George M. Cohan, the patriotic vaudevillian), with Joan Leslie, Walter Huston, Jeanne Cagney, Rosemary de Camp, S. Z. Sakall, George Barbier, Walter Catlett, Frances

Rehearsing with Alan Hale for *Captain of the Clouds* **(1942).**

125

Langford, Minor Watson and Eddie Foy Jr

Johnny Come Lately
(1943) William Cagney Production for United Artists. 97 minutes
Director William K. Howard *Screenplay* John Van Druten, from Louis Bromfield's book, McLeod's Folly) *Cast* James Cagney (as Tom Richards, a hobo journalist campaigning against corruption) with Grace George, Marjorie Main, Marjorie Lord, Hattie McDaniel, Edward McNamara, Bill Henry, Robert Barrat, George Cleveland and Margaret Hamilton

Blood on the Sun
(1945) William Cagney Productions for United Artists. 98 minutes
Director Frank Lloyd *Screenplay* Lester Cole and Nathaniel Curtis *Cast* James Cagney (as Nick Condon, a newspaper man in the Tokyo court of Baron Tanaka) with Sylvia Sidney, Wallace Ford, Rosemary de Camp, Robert Armstrong, John Emery, Leonard Strong and Frank Puglia

13 Rue Madeleine
(1946) 20th Century-Fox. 95 minutes
Director Henry Hathaway *Screenplay* John Monks Jr. and Sy Bartlett *Cast* James Cagney (as Bob Sharkey, an heroic American spy), with Annabella, Richard Conte, Frank Latimore, Walter Abel, Melville Cooper, Sam Jaffe, Marcel Rousseau and Richard Gordon

The Time of Your Life
(1948) William Cagney Productions for United Artists. 109 minutes
Director H. C. Potter *Screenplay* Nathaniel Curtis, from William Saroyan's play *Cast* James Cagney (as Joe, the champagne-swilling philosopher) with William Bendix, Wayne Morris, Jeanne Cagney, Broderick Crawford, Ward Bond, James Barton, Paul Draper, Gale Page, James Lydon, Richard Erdman, Pedro de Cordoba, Reginald Beane and Tom Powers

White Heat
(1949) Warner Bros. 114 minutes
Director Raoul Walsh *Screenplay* Ivan Goff and Ben Roberts, from Virginia Kellogg's story *Cast* James Cagney (as Cody Jarrett, manic hoodlum) with Virginia Mayo, Edmund O'Brien, Margaret Wycherley, Steve Cochran, John Archer, Wally Cassell and Mickey Knox

West Point Story
(1950) Warner Bros. 107 minutes
Director Roy Del Ruth *Screenplay* John Monks Jr., Charles Hoffman and Irving Wallace *Cast* James Cagney (as Elwin Bixby, a brash Broadway musical director) with Virginia Mayo, Doris Day, Gordon MacRae, Gene Nelson, Alan

Hale Jr., Roland Winters and Raymond Roe

Kiss Tomorrow Goodbye
(1950) William Cagney Productions for Warner Bros. 102 minutes
Director Gordon Douglas *Screenplay* Harry Brown, from Horace McCoy's novel *Cast* James Cagney (as Ralph Cotter, a vicious gangster who tricks the corrupt police of a big city) with Barbara Payton, Ward Bond, Luther Adler, Helena Carter, Steve Brodie, Rhys Williams and Barton MacLane

Come Fill the Cup
(1951) Warner Bros. 113 minutes
Director Gordon Douglas *Screenplay* Ivan Goff and Ben Roberts, from Harlan Ware's novel *Cast* James Cagney (as Lew Marsh, drunken anti-alcohol campaigning journalist) with Phyllis Thaxter, Raymond Massey, James Gleason, Gig Young, Selena Royle, Larry Keating and Charlita

Starlift
(1951) Warner Bros. 103 minutes
Director Roy Del Ruth *Screenplay* John Klorer and Karl Kamb *Cast* James Cagney (as himself) with Doris Day, Gordon MacRae, Virginia Mayo, Gene Nelson, Ruth Roman, Janice Rule, Dick Wesson, Ron Hagerty, Louella Parsons, Gary Cooper, Randolph Scott and Jane Wyman

What Price Glory?
(1952) 20th Century-Fox. 111 minutes
Director John Ford *Screenplay* Phoebe and Henry Ephron, from Maxwell Anderson and Laurence Stallings' play *Cast* James Cagney (as Captain Flagg, a comic army officer) with Corinne Calvet, Dan Dailey, William Demarest, Craig Hill, Robert Wagner, James Gleason, Marisa Pavan and Casey Adams

A Lion is in the Streets
(1953) William Cagney Productions for Warner Bros. 88 minutes
Director Raoul Walsh *Screenplay* Luther Davis, from Adria Locke Langley's novel. *Cast* James Cagney (as Hank Martin, a crooked lawyer politician) with Frank McHugh, Barbara Hale, Jeanne Cagney, Anne Francis, Warner Anderson, Lon Chaney Jr., Larry Keating and John McIntire

Run for Cover
(1955) Pine-Thomas/Paramount. 92 minutes
Director Nicholas Ray *Screenplay* Winston Miller *Cast* James Cagney (as Matt Dow, a sheriff in a small western town) with Viveca Lindfors, John Derek, Grant Withers, Jean Hersholt, Jack Lambert, Ernest Borgnine, Ray Teal and Irving Bacon

Love Me Or Leave Me
(1955) Metro-Goldwyn-Mayer. 122 minutes
Director Charles Vidor

Screenplay Daniel Fuchs and Isobel Lennart *Cast* James Cagney (as Martin 'The Gimp' Snyder, racketeer) with Doris Day, Cameron Mitchell, Robert Keith, Tom Tully, Harry Bellaver, Richard Gaines, Peter Leeds, Claude Stroud and Audrey Young

Mister Roberts
(1955) Warner Bros. 123 minutes
Directors John Ford, Mervyn LeRoy *Screenplay* Frank Nugent and Joshua Logan, from Logan and Thomas Heggan's play *Cast* James Cagney (as the obstinate captain of a naval ship on the edge of mutiny) with Henry Fonda, William Powell, Jack Lemmon, Ward Bond, Betsy Palmer, Phil Carey, Harry Carey Jr., Nick Adams, Ken Curtis and Frank Aletter

The Seven Little Foys
(1955) Paramount. 93 minutes
Director Melville Shavelson *Screenplay* Melville Shavelson and Jack Rose *Cast* James Cagney (as George M. Cohan) with Milly Vitale, George Tobias, Angela Clarke, Herbert Hayes, Richard Shannon, Billy Gray, Lee Erickson, Paul De Rolf and Lydia Reed

Tribute to a Bad Man
(1956) Metro-Goldwyn-Mayer. 95 minutes
Director Robert Wise *Screenplay* Michael Blankfort, from Jack Schaefer's short story *Cast* James Cagney (as Jeremy Rodock, a hang-'em-high cattle baron) with Irene Papas, Don Dubbins, Stephen McNally, Vic Morrow, James Griffith, James Bell, Lee Van Cleef and Onslow Stevens

These Wilder Years
(1956) Metro-Goldwyn-Mayer. 91 minutes
Director Roy Rowland *Screenplay* Frank Fenton *Cast* James Cagney (as Steve Bradford, a tycoon who goes in search of his illegitimate son) with Barbara Stanwyck, Walter Pidgeon, Betty Lou Keim, Don Dubbins, Edward Andrews, Basil Ruysdael, Grandon Rhodes and Will Wright

Man of a Thousand Faces
(1957) Universal-International. 122 minutes
Director Joseph Pevney *Screenplay* R. Wright Campbell, Ivan Goff and Ben Roberts *Cast* James Cagney (as silent screen star, Lon Chaney) with Dorothy Malone, Jane Greer, Marjorie Rambeau, Jim Backus, Robert J. Evans, Celia Lovsky and Jeanne Cagney

Short Cut to Hell
(1957) Paramount. 87 minutes
Director James Cagney *Screenplay* Ted Berkman and Raphael Blau, from W. R. Burnett's adaptation of Graham Greene's novel, A Gun For Sale *Cast* Robert Ivers, Georgann Johnson, William Bishop, Jacques Aubuchon, Peter Baldwin, Yvette Vickers and

Milton Frome with a short prologue by James Cagney

Never Steal Anything Small
(1958) Universal-International. 94 minutes
Director Charles Lederer *Screenplay* Charles Lederer, from Rouben Mamoulian and Maxwell Anderson's unproduced musical, Devil's Hornpipe *Cast* James Cagney (as Jake MacIllaney, a crooked stevedore in a union war) with Shirley Jones, Roger Smith, Cara Williams, Nehemiah Persoff, Royal Dano, Anthony Caruso, Horace MacMahon and Virginia Vincent

Shake Hands With the Devil
(1959) Pennebaker for United Artists. 110 minutes
Director Michael Anderson *Screenplay* Ivan Goff and Ben Roberts, from Marian Thompson's adaptation of Reardon Connor's novel. *Cast* James Cagney (as Sean Lenihan, a rebel doctor who fights for Irish Home Rule) with Don Murray, Dana Wynter, Glynis Johns, Michael Redgrave, Sybil Thorndike, Cyril Cusack, Harry Corbett, John Breslin, Harry Brogan, Richard Harris, Alan Cuthbertson, Robert Brown and John Le Mesurier

The Gallant Hours
(1960) Cagney-Montgomery Productions for United Artists. 115 minutes
Director Robert Montgomery *Screenplay* Beirne Lay Jr. and Frank D. Gilroy *Cast* James Cagney (as Admiral 'Bull' Halsey, Second World War hero) with Dennis Weaver, Ward Costello, Les Tremayne, Robert Burton, Richard Jaeckel, Raymond Bailey, Carl Benton Reid, James Cagney Jr. and Robert Montgomery Jr.

One, Two, Three
(1961) Mirisch/Pyramid, for United Artists. 108 minutes
Director Billy Wilder *Screenplay* Billy Wilder and I. A. L. Diamond, from Ferenc Molnar's one-act play *Cast* James Cagney (as C. P. MacNamara, the upwardly mobile Coca Cola tycoon) with Horst Buchholz, Pamela Tiffin, Arlene Francis, Lilo Pulver, Howard St. John, Hanns Lothar, Leon Askin and Red Buttons

Ragtime
(1981) Sunley Holdings Ltd. 155 minutes
Director Milos Forman *Screenplay* Michael Weller *Cast* James Cagney (as New York Police Commissioner Rheinlander Waldo, the ageing hardliner on the force), with Brad Dourif, Moses Gunn, Elizabeth McGovern, Kenneth McMillan, Pat O'Brien, Donald O'Connor, James Olson, Mary Steenburgen, Howard E. Rollins, Debbie Allen, Robert Joy and Norman Mailer.

Fresh mutts Cagney and Blondell.

Proteus would like to thank the following for
their help in supplying photographs:

The Kobal Collection: 2, 4, 10, 21, 31, 32, 35, 36, 38, 39,
40, 43, 45, 47, 50, 51, 52, 55, 57, 61, 62, 64, 68,
69, 76, 79, 84, 87, 88, 89, 92, 94, 96, 97, 102, 103,
105, 106, 108, 110, 111, 120, 121, 124, 125, 127

The British Film Archive Stills Library:
13, 22, 27, 28, 29, 51, 58, 72, 73, 78, 81, 82

Aquarius, London: 14, 98, 101, 112, 114, 127

David Edwards: 112